Henry Richard Linderman

Money and legal Tender in the United States

Henry Richard Linderman

Money and legal Tender in the United States

ISBN/EAN: 9783743317406

Manufactured in Europe, USA, Canada, Australia, Japa

Cover: Foto ©ninafisch / pixelio.de

Manufactured and distributed by brebook publishing software (www.brebook.com)

Henry Richard Linderman

Money and legal Tender in the United States

MONEY

AND

LEGAL TENDER

IN THE

UNITED STATES

BY

H. R. LINDERMAN

DIRECTOR OF THE MINT

NEW YORK
G. P. PUTNAM'S SONS
182 FIFTH AVENUE
1877

COPYRIGHT,
1877,
BY G. P. PUTNAM'S SONS.

PREFACE.

VARIOUS questions connected with the subject of Money and Legal Tender in the United States are receiving the earnest and careful consideration of the public. This is especially the case with respect to the question whether the full legal-tender coins shall be gold only, or both gold and silver in a relative valuation of the two metals fixed by law.

For about seventeen years the money in circulation has been (except as to the States of California and Nevada, where the gold standard has been maintained), United States Legal-Tender Notes based on the credit and resources of the nation, and National Bank Notes secured by a deposit of United States Bonds; and neither of these descriptions of notes redeemable in coin.

Until recently, the subject of bringing this currency from a credit to a specie basis has not received the attention which its great importance demands.

It is evident now, however, that we are on the eve of a thorough discussion of the subject in all its bearings. Properly to investigate United States money, reference must be made to the laws relating to coinage, legal tender, and the money standard.

No publication, that I am aware of, contains this information in brief and convenient form. To meet this requirement is the object of the work now given to the public, which, it is proper to say, has been prepared hurriedly, amidst the cares and duties of my official position. The views which it contains are my own, and for them I alone am responsible. If it shall be found useful to the public in the examination of questions so closely connected with our depressed industrial and business interests, and the future prosperity of the country, it will be a source of satisfaction to me, and more than repay the labor bestowed in its preparation.

WASHINGTON, D. C.,
June, 1877.

CONTENTS.

CHAPTER I.
BRIEF EXPLANATION OF TERMS COMMONLY USED IN TREATING OF BULLION, MINTS, COINAGE AND MONEY.

    Assaying, refining, etc., - - - 1

CHAPTER II.
AUTHORITY TO COIN MONEY AND REGULATE ITS VALUE IN THE UNITED STATES OF AMERICA.

    Government under the Articles of Confederation, 7

    Provisions of the Constitution of the United States as to Coinage, Legal Tender, Weights and Measures, - - - - - 8

    Legal Tender of base metal coins, - - 12

    The result of enlarging the limited tender of subsidiary silver coins, - - - - 12

    Constitution does not confer upon Congress the right to make paper a legal tender, - - - 13

CHAPTER III.
LEGISLATION REGULATING THE VALUE OF FOREIGN COINS.

    Act of July 31, 1789, - - - - 15

CHAPTER IV.

METALLIC MONEY IN COLONIAL TIMES AND UNDER THE CONFEDERATION.

	Page.
Colonial money of account,	18
Establishment of the dollar,	19
Divisions of the money of account,	20
Silver under-valued,	20

CHAPTER V.

ESTABLISHMENT OF THE MINT, MONEY STANDARD, NATIONAL COINAGE, MONEY OF ACCOUNT, AND LEGAL TENDER.

Act of April 2, 1792,	23
Standard adopted for gold and silver,	24
Change in the weight of the dollar,	26
Acts changing the weight and fineness of gold coins,	27
Silver three-cent piece authorized,	28

CHAPTER VI.

MONEY STANDARD 1792 TO 1853.

Review of legislation relative to gold and silver,	29

CHAPTER VII.

WITHDRAWAL AND RE-COINAGE OF FRACTIONAL SPANISH AND MEXICAN SILVER COINS.

Act of February 21, 1857,	32
Copper and other minor coinage,	33
Copper-nickel and bronze cents authorized,	34
Two-cent bronze and five-cent and three-cent minor coins authorized,	35
Redemption of minor coins,	35

CHAPTER VIII.

COINAGE-CHARGE, SEIGNIORAGE, GAIN FROM THE MANUFACTURE AND ISSUE OF MINOR COINS.

 Charge for coining and for making bars, -   -   37
 Purchase of bullion for subsidiary coins,   -   38
 Charge for coining gold abrogated,   -   -   39

CHAPTER IX.

COINAGE ACT OF 1873. CHANGE FROM THE DOUBLE STANDARD OF GOLD AND SILVER TO THE GOLD STANDARD.

 Mint established at Philadelphia,   -   -   40
 Made a Bureau of the Treasury Department,   -   41
 Trade dollar authorized,   -   -   -   42
 Relative value of gold and silver, -   -   -   43
 Demonetization of silver,   -   -   -   44
 Coinage of twenty-cent piece of silver authorized   45

CHAPTER X.

THE TRADE DOLLAR.

 Production of silver and market for the same,   47
 Old silver dollar not well received in China,   -   49
 Mexican dollar practically the money of account in China and Japan,   -   -   -   -   51
 New dollar for trade purposes proposed,   -   52
 Comparison of values,   -   -   -   -   54
 Reports of leading foreign banks,   -   -   57

CHAPTER XI.

GOLD IN THE FORM OF MINT-BARS AUTHORIZED TO BE HELD AND EXCHANGED BY THE ASSISTANT TREASURER AT NEW YORK.

 Act of January 22, 1874, - ,   -   -   -   60

CHAPTER XII.
COINAGE FOR FOREIGN STATES AT THE MINTS OF THE UNITED STATES.

Act of January 29, 1874, - - - 62

CHAPTER XIII.
LEGAL TENDER.

What constitutes legal tender, - - - 64

CHAPTER XIV.
PAR OF EXCHANGE AND VALUE OF FOREIGN COINS.

What constitutes mint par of exchange, - 66
Valuation of foreign coins, - - - 67
Extracts from Report of Senator Sherman on International Coinage, - - - - 70
Act to establish the custom-house value of the sovereign or pound sterling of Great Britain, and to fix the par of exchange, - - - 72
Value in our money terms of the money units of the various nations of the world, - - 75

CHAPTER XV.
PAPER CURRENCY SINCE 1863.

Issue of legal-tender notes on the credit of the United States, - - - - - 77

CHAPTER XVI.
ISSUE OF FRACTIONAL NOTES.

Issue of postage and revenue stamps as postal currency, - - - - - 80
Fractional notes substituted, - - - 80

CHAPTER XVII.
COIN CERTIFICATES.
Authorized by Act of March 3, 1863, - - 82

CHAPTER XVIII.
NATIONAL CURRENCY SECURED BY A PLEDGE OF UNITED STATES STOCKS.
Important features of the Act, - - - 84

CHAPTER XIX.
LEGISLATION FOR FUNDING AND EVENTUAL PAYMENT OF THE OBLIGATIONS OF THE UNITED STATES IN COIN.
Authorized by Act of February 25, 1862, - 86
Retirement and cancellation of United States notes, 87

CHAPTER XX.
MINT WEIGHTS AND WEIGHING OF BULLION AND COIN.
Old mint-weights, - - - - 93
Standard troy pound, - - - - 94
Castilian mark, - - - - 95
Tolerance for weight, - - - 96
Carat system, - - - - - 97
Metric system, - - - - - 98

CHAPTER XXI.
PROPOSITION FOR THE RE-MONETIZATION OF SILVER CONSIDERED.
Restoration of the old silver dollar, - - 100
Double standard ratio of 1 to $15\frac{1}{2}$, - - 101

	Page.
Statement of the money-standard question,	103
Position of France in connection with money-standard question,	107
Seigniorage on coinage should accrue to the Government,	110
Various ratios considered,	111
Probable result of coining silver dollars,	112
Act to "Strengthen the Public credit,"	113
Act to "Authorize the Re-funding of the National debt,"	114
Metallic money-standard should not be appreciated or depreciated by law,	117
Review of the money situation in Europe,	120
Amount of coin in the United States,	120

APPENDIX.

AGGREGATE PRODUCTION OF SILVER,	125
GENERAL SUMMARY OF THE MOVEMENTS OF SILVER,	131
USE OF SILVER FOR PURPOSES OF MANUFACTURE,	133
NATIONS AND POPULATIONS UNDER THE THREE SYSTEMS (GOLD; GOLD AND SILVER; SILVER),	143
THE RIGHT TO COIN MONEY,	152
COINS OF THE UNITED STATES, AUTHORITY FOR COINING AND CHANGES IN WEIGHT AND FINENESS,	155
THE RATIOS OF GOLD TO SILVER FROM 1760 TO 1833,	160
YEARLY AVERAGES OF THE PRICE OF SILVER FROM 1834 TO 1876, ETC.,	161
TOTAL COINAGE OF THE UNITED STATES MINTS TO JUNE 30, 1877,	163

MONEY AND LEGAL TENDER

IN THE

UNITED STATES.

CHAPTER I.

BRIEF EXPLANATION OF TERMS COMMONLY USED IN TREATING OF BULLION, MINTS, COINAGE, AND MONEY.

ASSAYING.—Chemical analysis of metals or ores. This term, as employed in reference to mints and coinage, refers particularly to the processes for determining the component parts and relative proportions of a mixed alloy of gold and silver, or of the various alloys used for the manufacture of minor coins.

Refining.—Extraction of base from precious metals; usually performed by the aid of heat and oxidizing fluxes.

Parting.—The separation of gold and silver when the two metals compose an alloy, either native or artificial, for the purpose of obtaining the metals respectively in the form of fine bars. This is accomplished, first, by dissolving the silver with acids and subsequently precipitating; or, second, by converting silver into a chloride by heat and chlorine gas, and then reducing the chloride to a metallic state.

Alloying.—Compounding two or more metals together in suitable or legal proportions for coinage. Gold and silver are alloyed with copper for standard coins, and alloys are variously made of nickel and copper, or of copper, tin, and zinc for minor coins.

Fine Bars.—Gold or silver bars resulting from the operations of parting and refining. Bars containing 99 per cent. of pure metal are generally considered as fine bars.

Unparted Bullion.—Gold containing silver, or silver containing gold, which has not been subjected to the parting operation.

Amalgam.—Gold or silver extracted from ores or other substances by the use of mercury, and left in a porous or spongy condition when the mercury is removed by distillation.

Fineness.—A term indicating the proportion of pure metal contained in a piece of gold or silver. Fineness is expressed in thousandths: that is, pure metal is 1000 fine. United States coin is $\frac{900}{1000}$ fine, or, decimally, .900 fine. Fineness is estimated by jewelers and workers in the precious metals by "carats," pure metal being 24 carats. Thus, 22 carats, the British standard for gold coins, is $\frac{22}{24}$, or, decimally, .916$\frac{2}{3}$ fine.

Deposit-Melting.—The operation of melting a deposit of gold or silver at the mint to secure a homogeneity of metals preliminary to taking a sample for assaying.

Remedy of the Mint.—The legal variation allowed from the fineness and weight prescribed by law for the coins.

Trial of the Pyx.—The annual test, made by special commissioners, of the fineness and weight of coins reserved from each delivery of coin by the coiner to the superintendent. These coins are known as Pyx Coins because kept in a pyx, or chest.

Refractory Bullion.—Gold or silver bullion which contains a small percentage of lead, tin or antimony, and which is therefore too hard or brittle to roll, cut or stamp, with facility.

Wastage.—The amount of gold and silver lost in the processes which the metals undergo preparatory to striking the coins. This "wastage" by law must not exceed a certain percentage of the gross amount of metals worked.

Sweepings.—The ashes, fluxes, crucibles, sweepings and all other refuse materials from rooms in which the metals are worked, containing a small amount of gold and silver.

Seigniorage.—In modern times, the difference between the actual or bullion value of coins and their nominal or tale value; retained by some governments as a mint charge for coinage.

Standard.—The weight and fineness fixed by law for the coins. Hence the terms "standard weight" and "standard fineness" for coins.

Base Bullion.—Gold or silver bullion not fit for coinage purposes by reason of the presence of base metals until refined.

Mint-Mark.—The letter or mark on the coin designating the mint at which it was struck: as "S" for San Francisco; "C. C." for Carson City.

Money of Account.—The ideal unit, or money term in which accounts are stated or transactions made, as the *Pound Sterling* of Great Britain, the *Dollar* of the United States, the *Franc* of France, and the *Reichsmark* of the German Empire.

Standard Coins, or Coins of Standard Value.—In modern times a government first establishes a money of account or ideal unit, and then fixes by law the quantity of gold or silver which shall, in the form of a coin with unlimited legal-tender power, represent that ideal unit. Such coins with their multiples and divisions are termed *standard coins, or coins of standard value.*

Where a government fixes a certain weight of gold, and a certain weight of silver, to represent respectively the ideal unit in full legal-tender coins, a ratio, or relative valuation, of the two metals in the coinage, or a double standard, is thereby established, and the coins of both metals are *standard coins.*

Subsidiary Coins.—In the United States, silver coins of less denomination than the dollar, which have a nominal value exceeding their intrinsic or bullion value, and limited as legal tender to sums not exceeding five dollars.

Minor Coins.—Coins of small denominations, used for change, and struck from other metals than gold or silver.

Coining Value, or Mint Price of Gold or Silver.—The rate per standard ounce at which the mint converts bullion into unlimited legal-tender coins.

The coining rate of an ounce of standard gold bullion—*i. e.* bullion $\frac{900}{1000}$ fine—in the United States is $18.604+.

The coining rate for the silver dollar of $412\frac{1}{2}$ grains, discontinued by law Apr. 1, 1873, was 1.16\frac{4}{11}$ per standard ounce.

The British coining rate is 1869 sovereigns for

forty (troy) pounds of sterling standard gold, or, £3 17s. 10½d. per ounce troy, British or sterling standard: that is, gold 22 carats ($\frac{11}{12}$), or .916⅔ fine.

Money Standard.—The basis of the money system of all civilized nations is Gold, or Silver, or both in a ratio fixed by law. These metals may accordingly be regarded as universal standards of value.

Where the ideal unit of the money of account is represented in unlimited legal-tender gold coin only, and the value and legal tender of silver coins is made subordinate to gold, the gold standard prevails; and where the money unit is represented in silver coins to the exclusion of gold as an unlimited legal tender, the silver standard prevails.

Where the unit is represented both by gold and silver coins of unlimited legal tender, with unrestricted coinage, the double standard prevails.

. The ratio, or relative valuation of the two metals, in the coins of nations employing the double standard is, at the present time, almost without exception, *one* of gold to *fifteen and a half* of silver.

CHAPTER II.

AUTHORITY TO COIN MONEY AND REGULATE ITS VALUE IN THE UNITED STATES OF AMERICA.

Government under the Articles of Confederation.

ARTICLE II. Each State retains its sovereignty, freedom, and independence, and every power, jurisdiction, and right, which is not by this Confederation expressly delegated to the United States in Congress assembled.

ARTICLE IX. The United States in Congress assembled shall also have the sole and exclusive right and power of regulating the alloy and value of coin struck by their own authority, or by that of the respective States. . . . The United States in Congress assembled shall have authority . . . to borrow money or emit bills on the credit of the United States.

Provisions of the Constitution of the United States as to Coinage, Legal Tender, Weights and Measures.

ART. I, SEC. 8. The Congress shall have power . . . to coin money, regulate the value thereof, and of foreign coins, and fix the standard of weights and measures, . . . to provide for the punishment of counterfeiting the securities and current coin of the United States.

ART. I, SEC. 10. No State shall . . . coin money, emit bills of credit, make anything but gold and silver coin a tender in payment of debts.

ART. I, SEC. 11. The powers not delegated to the United States by the Constitution, nor prohibited by it to the States, are reserved to the States respectively or to the people.

After the Declaration of Independence and before the adoption of the Articles of Confederation, each of the thirteen original States, had, as an attribute or incident of sovereignty, the right to coin money.

In the Articles of Confederation the States expressly delegated to the United States in Congress assembled, "the sole and exclusive right and power of regulating the alloy and value of coin, struck by their own authority or by that of the respective States."

Under this provision, the States retained the right to coin money concurrently with the Government of the Confederation, but only according to the standard of fineness, weight, and value prescribed by the central government.

The right to emit or issue paper money, known as "Bills of Credit," had been exercised by the several States, before the adoption of the Articles of Confederation, and by these, authority was given to the United States to issue such bills.

Paper money continued to be issued by the States, and was also issued by the Government of the Confederation under the authority delegated in the compact.

The object, in delegating to the United States the sole and exclusive right to regulate the alloy and value of coin, was to insure uniformity as to weight, fineness, and value throughout the several States.

Under the pressing necessities attending the transition of the colonies to independence, and again from this position of separate States to a united nation with a Republican Government, the issue of credit money was a matter of necessity. It was, under the circumstances, probably the most convenient and available means of financial support.

Before the establishment of a money system, the Confederation of States gave way to a Constitution, ordained and established by the people of the United States. The coinage of money and the regulation of what should be used in the payment of debts was placed under the exclusive control of the National Government. The coinage of money, emission of bills of credit, or the making of anything but gold and silver coin a tender in payment of debts, by any of the States of the Union, was expressly prohibited.

The grant of power to "coin money, regulate the value thereof, and of foreign coins," although only briefly outlined in the Constitution, obviously includes as means necessary to execute the same, the right to establish a money of account and to make coined money (gold and silver) a legal tender throughout the United States. The regulation of the value of money coined by the United States and of foreign coins is one thing, and the making of such coins a legal tender, another. The former fixes the value of a certain weight of metal, and the latter renders it obligatory on every one to receive it at that valuation in payment of debts.

The purpose of this grant of power to Congress, and the prohibition to the States (as to the coinage and issue of money, or the making of anything but gold and silver coin a legal tender,) was unquestionably to place the subject under the control of Congress, without limitation or restriction.

The States may make gold and silver coin a legal tender, but if the right be exercised, it must be in conformity with, and subordinate to, the laws of the United States.

Under the power to coin money and regulate its value, Congress may make both gold and silver the standard or unlimited legal-tender money, and in a fixed relation; or, either may be selected for that purpose, leaving the other in a subordinate position; and this cannot be regarded as in any way interfering with the implied right of the States to make gold and silver coin a tender in payment of debts. The gold and silver coin which they may make a tender must be the gold and silver coins of the United States, and foreign gold and silver coins, but only according to the legal-tender value thereof, as regulated by the laws of the United States.

The power to coin money embraces other metals than gold and silver, and consequently copper and alloys of different useful metals are coined into denominations representing the divisions (fractions) of the money of account, for which gold and silver are not adapted. A coin made of the precious metals to represent the hundredth part of a dollar would be too small in size for convenient use.

In the earlier Acts of Congress, authorizing the issue of cents and half-cents, there was no provision as to legal tender. It is probable that some doubts were at first entertained as to the power of Congress to make coins, composed of any other metals than gold and silver, legal tender.

The base-metal coins were first made a limited tender by law in 1864, previous to which they were, in effect, simply declared to be of the value stamped upon them.

If the States possessed any power whatever to alter the legal tender of coin, they might at any time seriously interfere with and disturb the money system established by Congress, to the great detriment of that uniform commercial system which it is the purpose of the Constitution to secure.

If Congress, in the exercise of its unlimited power to regulate the value of money, decides in favor of gold as a single standard, it necessarily places the silver coins in a subordinate position, both as to value and legal tender, and the legal-tender limit cannot be enlarged or removed by a State.

It is worth while to consider what the effect would be, if a State possessed and exercised the right of enlarging the limited tender fixed by United States law for the subsidiary silver coins. The first result would be the accumulation in that State of a great portion of the coinage intended by Congress to be used for change money throughout all the States. Secondly, the over-valued silver coin would at once expel the standard moneys from that State; and soon such State would find itself with a money system of its own different from that of all other States. Confusion in respect to contracts and all business would follow until it became intolerable and required an immediate repeal of the disturbing legislation.

In this connection it should be observed that there is not a line nor word in the Constitution which in terms gives Congress the right or power to make any thing but coined money a legal tender in payment of debts. There is no provision in that instrument under which the right is even implied, unless it be from the power "to raise and support armies."

Under this war power, the right to issue legal-tender paper money has been asserted and once exercised by the Government. The right, so exercised, has been sustained by the Supreme Court under the plea of necessity, of which necessity Congress is the judge. And the Government will exercise the power whenever the taxing and borrowing power are found insufficient to yield the means of suppressing an extensive rebellion, or repelling a formidable invasion.

Under the power granted to borrow money, Congress may authorize the issue of credit or demand notes, or other evidences of debt, and make the same receivable by the United States Treasury, and thereby aid in giving such notes currency as money, but it has no power to compel their acceptance in payment of private debts, except in the emergency of "necessity." This mode of borrowing money has been exercised at different times in our history.

Clothing with legal-tender power any money but coin is one of the most responsible acts of government. As a matter of equity to the people, the legal-tender attribute in respect to all issues outstanding should continue until such money be either funded or made redeemable in the standard metallic money.

CHAPTER III.

LEGISLATION REGULATING THE VALUE OF FOREIGN COINS.

AT the first session of the first Congress, which commenced, in the City of New York, March 4, 1789, under the provisions of the new Constitution, an Act was passed "for laying a duty on goods, wares and merchandizes imported into the United States." Also an Act to regulate the collection of duties, and for other purposes. In the latter Act, the value of foreign coins was regulated as follows:

ACT JULY 31, 1789.

"That all foreign coins and currencies shall be estimated according to the following rates: each pound sterling of Great Britain, at four dollars forty-four cents; each livre tournois of France, at eighteen cents and a half; each florin or guilden of the United Netherlands, at thirty-nine cents; each mark banco of Hamburg, at thirty-three cents and one third;

each rix dollar of Denmark, at one hundred cents; each rix dollar of Sweden, at one hundred cents; each rouble of Russia, at one hundred cents; each real plate of Spain, at ten cents; each milreis of Portugal at one dollar and twenty-four cents; each pound sterling of Ireland, at four dollars ten cents; each tale of China, at one dollar forty-eight cents; each pagoda of India, at one dollar ninety-four cents; each rupee of Bengal at fifty-five cents and a half; and all other denominations of money in value as near as may be to the said rates."

The value of these foreign coins was expressed in the terms of the money of account established by the Congress of the Confederation; and on their estimated value respectively as compared with the Spanish Dollar.

Different Acts regulating the value and legal tender of foreign gold and silver coins were afterwards passed, to which it is not necessary to refer in detail, as those coins have long since passed out of circulation. All the legislation upon the subject, except the Act of July 31, 1789, contemplated the substitution, as early as practicable, of a national coinage. The value at which various foreign coins were made a legal tender in United States money was, as a rule, a fraction less than their bullion value, the effect of which was to send them to the Mint for conversion into U. S. Coins. By the 3d section of the Act of Feb. 21, 1857, all former Acts authorizing the currency of foreign gold or silver coins, and declaring the same a legal tender in payment of debts, were repealed.

CHAPTER IV.

METALLIC MONEY IN COLONIAL TIMES AND UNDER THE CONFEDERATION.

DURING the period of our colonial history, and down to the time of the issue of national coinage under the Federal Constitution, gold and silver coins of different nations were in use in North America, but silver alone appears to have been legally recognized, for the reason, no doubt, that the silver standard prevailed generally.

The colonial money of account was originally an ideal unit called a pound, with divisions of shillings and pence. There was however no legal tender; but the Spanish dollar (silver) appears to have been the money generally used in coin-payments and universally current in the colonies. This dollar was in fact the principal coin of commerce at that time, and for many years before.

Each colony had its own paper currency, in which the value of the Spanish dollar was, in 1782, according to Robert Morris, "in Georgia, five shillings; North Carolina and New York, eight shillings; in Virginia and the four Eastern States, six shillings; in all the other States except South Carolina, seven shillings and six pence, and in South Carolina, thirty-two shillings and six pence."

In computations of exchange with England the Spanish dollar was uniformly estimated at four shillings six pence—or fifty-four pence,—sterling.

The rate of $4s.$ $6d.$ sterling was based on assays made at the London mint of pieces in circulation previous to 1717, according to which these dollars contained $386\frac{3}{4}$ grains fine silver.

According to the British standard, established in 1601, 444 grains of fine silver were rated at $5s.$ $2d.$ sterling, and, therefore, $4s.$ $6d.$ was represented by $386\frac{7}{10}$ grains.

In 1728 the fine silver in the Spanish dollar was reduced by law to $383\frac{2}{10}$ grains and in 1772 to $374\frac{1}{8}$ grains.

In Congress, July 6, 1785, the dollar was established as the ideal money unit of the United States of America. On the 8th of August, 1786, it was enacted that the standard for coinage of gold and of silver should be 11 parts fine and one part alloy, and the money unit or dollar should contain $375\frac{64}{100}$ grains fine silver.

The divisions of the money of account were, by the same enactment, denominated dollars, dimes, cents, and mills, and the following coins authorized:

Silver.	Dollar,	$375\frac{64}{100}$	grains fine silver.
	Half-dollar,	$187\frac{82}{100}$	" " "
	Double-dime,	$75\frac{128}{1000}$	" " "
	Dime,	$37\frac{564}{1000}$	" " "
Copper.	Cent,	$157\frac{1}{2}$	" copper.
	Half-cent,	$78\frac{3}{4}$	" "
Gold.	Eagle, (ten dollars),	$246\frac{268}{1000}$	grains fine gold.
	Half-eagle (five dollars),	$123\frac{134}{1000}$	" " "

The intention, in fixing the quantity of fine silver in the monetary unit, was to conform to the estimated average content of fine silver in the Spanish dollar then in circulation in this country.

The ratio of gold and silver in the coins thus authorized was 1 to 15.253. The market relation of the two metals was at that time 1 to $14\frac{89}{100}$. In the ratio prescribed for the coinage, silver was undervalued to the extent of nearly $2\frac{1}{2}$ per cent.

The object of this undervaluation of silver cannot now be ascertained.

Silver, as before stated, was then, as it had been for a long period before, the principal money of commerce, and supplies of that metal were much more likely to be received than gold.

Gold and silver were, at that time, undiscovered in the territory of the United States. The reliance for the needed supply was upon other countries, in exchange for commodities.

The ratio, or relative valuation, established was not calculated to insure the concurrent circulation of gold and silver coins, yet this, it appears, was contemplated.

Comparatively nothing was accomplished, during the brief life of the Confederation, in carrying into effect the resolutions of Congress in respect to a mint or coinage.

The accounts of Robert Morris, Financier of the Confederation, show that he expended about two thousand dollars for the establishment of "The Mint of North America,"* and that his efforts ended with the manufacture of three or four dies for the copper

---

* The origin of the United States Treasury seal is unknown. The translation of the Latin legend is, "Seal of the Treasury of North America."

Robert Morris used the term, "Mint of North America," and the charter of the "Bank of North America" emanated from him.

In the proceedings of public assemblies, as well as in newspapers and letters of the period of the Confederation, the words "Continental Army," "Continental Congress," "Continental Money," appear to have been uniformly used in making reference to public affairs. As the words used by Mr. Morris in the charter of the National Bank granted by the Congress of the Confederation, and those designating the mint authorized by the same authority, are identical with those in the legend of the Treasury seal, it is probable that the latter was prepared under his direction whilst occupying the office of Financier of the Confederation.

coinage. While a number of pieces were struck, no regular issue of coin took place.

The Government of the Confederation sought to withdraw the depreciated, almost worthless, paper currency, and establish a metallic money system, but the difficulties in the way, arising from the impoverished condition of the country, and deranged state of its industries, rendered this impossible.

CHAPTER V.

ESTABLISHMENT OF THE MINT, MONEY STANDARD, NATIONAL COINAGE, MONEY OF ACCOUNT, AND LEGAL TENDER.

THE Act of April 2, 1792, established the Mint, also the money of account, and authorized a National Coinage.

The ideal unit of the money of account was the Dollar divided into dimes or tenths, cents or hundreths, and mills or thousandths.

The money standard established by this Act was Gold and Silver, in the ratio or relative valuation of 1 to 15. The gold coins authorized to be struck were the eagle, half-eagle, and quarter-eagle, of the declared value of ten, five, and two and a half dollars, respectively; silver coins, the dollar, half-dollar, quarter-dollar and dime; copper coins, the cent and half-cent.

The gold and silver coins were made legal tender without limit, and the coinage thereof was free to all persons depositing bullion at the mint.

The copper coins were not made a legal tender, but were in effect simply declared to be of the value inscribed upon their face.

The standard for the silver coins was one thousand four hundred and eighty-five parts fine, to one hundred and seventy-nine parts alloy, the alloy to consist wholly of copper. This standard corresponds to 892.43 thousandths, and was retained until the end of the year 1836, when the silver coinage was intermitted, in anticipation of the passage of the Act of January 18, 1837, which changed the standard to 900 thousandths.

The fineness of eleven-twelfths was adopted for the gold coinage: that is to say, the coins were to be composed of eleven parts of pure gold to one of alloy. The alloy of the gold coins to be composed of silver and copper not exceeding one-half silver, as might be found convenient. This standard corresponds to twenty-two carats, or to 916.66 .. thousandths. The alloy was not valued in either the gold or silver coinage.

The standard weight and content of pure metal in the coins were as follows:

	STAND. WEIGHT.	PURE GOLD.
Eagle,	270 grs. troy.	247½ grs. troy.
Half-eagle,	135 " "	123¾ " "
Quarter-eagle,	67½ " "	61⅞ " "

	STAND. WEIGHT.	PURE SILVER.
Dollar,	416 " "	$371\frac{1}{4}$ grs. troy.
Half-dollar,	208 " "	$185\frac{5}{8}$ " "
Quarter-dollar,	104 " "	$92\frac{13}{16}$ " "
Dime,	$41\frac{3}{5}$ " "	$37\frac{1}{8}$ " "
Half-dime,	$20\frac{4}{5}$ " "	$18\frac{9}{16}$ " "
Weight of copper cent,	264 " "	
" " half-cent,	132 " "	

The variation from standard or "remedy of the mint" allowed in the gold and silver coins was one part in one hundred and forty-four parts.

In the recent gold coinage, the alloy is almost exclusively copper, the silver contained being less than one tenth of the alloy, while gold coins in existence at the time of the enactment of the original coinage Act (1792), contained a larger percentage of silver.

The change is due to the improvements which have since been made in the art of parting and refining bullion, by which nearly all the silver contained in gold as it comes from the mines can be profitably separated. It should be noted, in this connection, that Alexander Hamilton, in determining the quantity of pure silver for the dollar, did not take the lawful standard of the Spanish dollar of any particular issue, nor the average of the different issues, as his guide, but the actual average content of fine silver in the Spanish dollars then in circulation, which coin had, for many years previously been, as it was then, the standard by which other moneys were generally measured, and in which contracts and money obligations in this country were discharged.

The Dollar or Unit adopted in 1786, by the Congress of the Confederation, was to contain $375\tfrac{64}{100}$ grains pure silver. Before any coinage took place, the intrinsic or bullion value of the Unit was altered by the following provision in the Mint Act of 1792: "There shall be, from time to time, struck and coined at the said Mint, Dollars or Units, each to be of the value of a Spanish milled dollar, as the same is now current, and to contain $371\tfrac{1}{4}$ grains of pure, or 416 grains of standard, silver." The average quantity of fine silver contained in the Spanish dollars then in circulation in this country, was, according to the assay of a number of pieces, 371 grains, to which was added $\tfrac{1}{4}$ of a grain to avoid inconvenient fractions, in prescribing the weight of the coins under the ratio of 1 to 15.

In taking this course in reference to the coined dollar, Mr. Hamilton no doubt had in mind the importance of exact justice between debtors and creditors, and recognized the principle that a government, in fixing a money standard, cannot with justice depreciate the existing measure of contracts to the injury of creditors, or appreciate it to the detriment of debtors.

The Monetary Act of 1792 continued in force and without modification or amendment until June 28, 1834, when an Act was passed prescribing the following weights for the gold coins respectively:

	STAND. WEIGHT.	PURE GOLD.
Eagle, value $10,	258 grains.	232 grains.
Half-eagle, value $5,	129 "	116 "
Quarter-eagle, value $2.50,	64½ "	58 "

This Act further provided that said gold coins should be received in all payments, when of full weight, according to their respective values; and when of less than full weight, at less value, proportioned to their actual respective weights.

The standard fineness of the above coins, was 899.225 thousandths, and was retained until changed to 900 thousandths by the act of January 18, 1837. The weights of the gold coins were not, however, altered by this last Act;* and all gold coins made after July 31, 1834, are legal tenders according to their nominal values.

* The fineness, it will be remarked, was fractionally advanced, whereby the contents, fine, of the coins became

Eagle,	232.2 grains.
Half-eagle,	116.1 "
Quarter-eagle,	58.05 "

and the new coins in proportion as follows:

Dollar,	25.8 grains standard,	23.22 grains fine.
Double-eagle,	516 " "	464.40 " "
Three-dollar piece,	77.4 " "	69.66 " "

The coinage of double-eagles and gold dollar-pieces, or units, was authorized by the Act of March 3, 1849, and the three-dollar piece by the Act of February 21, 1853.

The Act of March 3, 1851, authorized the coinage of "a piece of the demomination and legal value of three cents or three hundredths of a dollar," composed of three-fourths silver and one-fourth copper (750 thousandths fine,) and to weigh $12\frac{3}{8}$ grains. The same Act made this piece a legal tender for all sums of thirty cents and under. By the Act of March 3, 1853, the fineness of this piece was increased to 900 thousandths, and the weight reduced to $11\frac{52}{100}$ grains, by which it was brought into conformity with the standard of the silver coins of less denominations than the dollar as fixed by the Act of February 21, 1853. This coin was discontinued under the provisions of the Coinage Act of 1873.

The coinage of this piece was authorized for the purpose of providing a postal currency, and it was stamped at a rate above its bullion value sufficient to prevent its being melted down or exported.

CHAPTER VI.

MONEY STANDARD 1792 TO 1853.

THE brief account of the legislation in relation to gold and silver money, from the organization of the Government under the Constitution of the United States down to the commencement of the late civil war, given in the preceding pages, exhibits the following features:

1. The adoption in 1792 of a gold and silver standard on a ratio or relative valuation of 15 to 1, which ratio corresponded substantially with the market relation of the two metals at that time.

2. A reduction in 1834 and 1837 of the weight and fineness of the gold coins by which the ratio or relative valuation of gold and silver in the coinage was fixed at 1 to 15.988, instead of 1 to 15.

This change increased the coining rate or legal-tender value of gold in this country $6\frac{589}{1000}$ per cent., and was made because for several years previous gold had been worth more in the markets of the world than its valuation in United States coins.

The author of the coinage law of 1792, Hamilton, assumed that in the markets of Europe one ounce of pure gold was equal in value to fifteen ounces of pure silver, which appears to have been the fact; but within a few years thereafter this relative value of the two metals changed, so that an ounce of pure gold was equal in value to $15\frac{1}{2}$ or 16 ounces of pure silver.

Gold being undervalued in United States coins, the latter found their way to markets where gold commanded more than the value stamped at the United States Mint. Congress undertook, in the year 1834, to remove this difficulty by a corresponding increase of the coining rate or value of gold.

3. It was soon apparent, however, that gold had been slightly overvalued by the new law, (1834). This overvaluation, and the fact that the coining rate of the two metals in the principal European countries was 1 to $15\frac{1}{2}$, gave silver a higher value in the market as bullion than its coining rate at the United States Mint. Concurrent circulation with gold could not be thereafter effectively maintained.

4. The difficulties experienced by this expulsion of the silver coins from the channels of circulation, especially those of small denominations, finally called for a new adjustment of the coinage, and, in 1853, the weight of the silver coins of less denomination than the dollar was reduced to an extent sufficient

to insure their retention in circulation, but their legal-tender quality was, at the same time, limited to the amount of five dollars.

The measures adopted in 1834 and 1853 in respect to the coinage were decided steps toward the establishment of a single gold standard, and were no doubt so intended.

CHAPTER VII.

WITHDRAWAL AND RE-COINAGE OF FRACTIONAL SPANISH AND MEXICAN SILVER COINS.

FOR many years prior to the reduction, in 1853, of the weight of United States silver coins of less denomination than the dollar, the pieces known as the quarter, eighth and sixteenth of the Spanish and Mexican dollar constituted a considerable portion of the change money of this country. From long use these pieces had become so worn that on the greater portion of them the inscriptions and devices were quite illegible, and their bullion value was thus reduced considerably below the nominal or tale value at which they were current by law and usage.

After an ample supply of United States silver coins of reduced weight and limited tender had been issued, there was no longer any excuse for allowing the worn and depreciated Spanish and Mexican fractional pieces to remain in circulation.

An Act was accordingly passed (Feb. 21, 1857),

repeating all former Acts making these foreign coins current or legal-tender money, and fixing the following rates at which they should be received at the Treasury of the United States, its several offices, and at the several post-offices and land-offices.

$\frac{1}{4}$ of a dollar or piece of two reals, 20 cents.
$\frac{1}{8}$ "   "   "   one   "   10 "
$\frac{1}{16}$ "   "   "   half "   5 "

These pieces had previously been current at twenty-five, twelve and a half, and six and a quarter cents respectively, or thereabouts.

When received at the Government offices, they were sent to the Mint for conversion into United States coin. They were also received at the Mint at their nominal values respectively, in exchange for the copper-nickel cents authorized by the same Act.

Under the foregoing provisions of law, the foreign fractional coins speedily found their way to the Mint, and in a few years disappeared from circulation.

Copper and other Minor Coinage.

Under the provisions of the Monetary Act of 1792, the coinage of copper cents of the weight of 264 grains, and half-cents of proportionate weight, was authorized.

The weight of the cent was, by the Act of June 14,

1793,—and before any regular copper coinage took place,—reduced to 208 grains; and by proclamation of the President, January 20, 1796, in conformity with an Act of March 3, 1795, it was further reduced to 168 grains.

The weight of the half-cent was, by the Act of January 14, 1793, reduced to 104 grains, and afterwards by the Proclamation and Act above referred to, the weight of the half-cent was further reduced to 84 grains. The reduction in weight was made on account of an increase in the price of copper, and also because the expenses of coinage proved to be greater than the first estimate.

The coinage of copper cents and half-cents was discontinued under the provisions of the Act of February 21, 1857, up to which time the total coinage was: Cents, $1,562,887.44; Half cents, $39,926.10.

The Act of February 21, 1857, authorized the coinage of a cent of 72 grains, composed of eighty-eight parts copper and twelve parts nickel. The Act of April 22, 1864, discontinued the coinage of this alloy and authorized the coinage of a one-cent piece, weighing 48 grains, composed of 95 per cent. copper and 5 per cent. tin and zinc.

The total amount of copper-nickel cents struck was $2,007,720, and of bronze, to close of fiscal year 1876, $1,697,065. The weight and alloy of the bronze cent has not since been changed, but remains as fixed by the Act of April 22, 1864, by which Act the coinage was authorized of a two-cent bronze piece of the same alloy, weighing 96 grains. This two-cent piece was discontinued by the Coinage Act of February 12, 1873.

The Act of March 3, 1865, authorized a three-cent coin, weighing 30 grains, composed of 75 parts copper and 25 parts nickel, and the Act of May 16, 1866, authorized a five-cent piece, weighing 77.16 grains, or 5 grams, metric system, composed of the same alloy, 75 parts copper and 25 parts nickel.

Both pieces continue to be coined; the amounts to close of fiscal year 1876 were, respectively, of the three-cent piece, $855,090, and of the five, $5,747,-840.

The Act of April 22, 1864, made the one-cent bronze coin a legal tender to the amount of ten cents, and the two-cent bronze piece to the amount of twenty cents.

Then, for the first time, was a legal-tender character given to coins composed of other metals than gold and silver. Following this precedent, the three-cent and five-cent copper-nickel pieces were made legal tenders in sums not exceeding sixty cents and one dollar, respectively. The legal tender of one-cent and two-cent coins was, by the Act of March 3, 1865, reduced to four cents.

A new and important feature in respect to minor

coins was the incorporation in the Act of May 16, 1866, of a provision requiring the United States Treasury "to redeem in national currency" the five-cent copper-nickel coins when presented in sums of not less than one hundred dollars.

The Act of March 3, 1865, discontinued the issue of fractional paper notes below the denomination of five cents, and that of May 16, 1866, notes of less denomination than ten cents, and provided for the withdrawal and cancellation of such issues.

No restriction was placed by law on the issue of the different token-coins, and the amount in circulation finally became redundant until much inconvenience arose therefrom, particularly to persons who, from the nature of their business, were compelled to receive numerous payments in small sums.

To provide a remedy for this evil, the Act of March 3, 1871, required the Secretary of the Treasury to redeem in lawful money all copper, bronze, copper-nickel, and base metal coinage of the United States. The same Act authorized the Secretary to discontinue, or diminish from time to time, the manufacture and issue of such coinage.

The five-cent and three-cent copper-nickel, and one-cent bronze coins, were, by the Coinage Act of 1873, made a legal tender, at their nominal value, for any amount not exceeding twenty-five cents in any one payment, and this is the existing law.

CHAPTER VIII.

COINAGE CHARGE, SEIGNIORAGE, GAIN FROM THE MANUFACTURE AND ISSUE OF MINOR COINS.

UNDER our mint system no charge or deduction whatever was made for the coinage of gold and silver prior to the Act of February 21, 1853, which took effect from and after July 1 of that year. This Act provided that "whether the gold and silver deposited be coined or cast into bars or ingots," there should be a charge to the depositor, (in addition to the charge made under previous laws for refining or parting the metals), of one-half of one per cent.

This applied to gold and silver bars, gold coin and silver dollars.

On the third of March following, the provisions of the above Act were modified so as to alter the charge of one-half per cent. for making bars to the actual cost of the operation.

The charge for making gold coins and silver dollars remained at one-half per cent. until April 1, 1873, when, under the provisions of the Coinage Act of that year, it was reduced to one-fifth of one per cent. for the gold coinage; the coinage of silver dollars had been, by the same Act, discontinued.

Although the cost of coining silver per dollar in value is probably about four times as great as that of gold, no difference was made in the charge for coining the two metals by the Act of 1853.

This was due, no doubt, to the provision made in the same Act, whereby all the silver coins, except the dollar piece, were thereafter to be coined on account of the Public Treasury, as well as to the belief entertained at the time that there would not be any considerable quantity of silver dollars coined, their bullion value being above their nominal or legal-tender value.

Under the provisions of the Act, the bullion required for the coinage of the half-dollar, quarter-dollar, dime, and half-dime, and the three-cent silver piece, was purchased, through the Mints, by the Treasury, and coined and issued on its account; the difference between the cost of the bullion including expense of manufacturing the coins, and their tale value, being the seigniorage or gain realized by the Government. No change in respect to the issue of these coins has since been made.

All copper, bronze, and copper-nickel coins have,

from the organization of the Mint down to the present time, been manufactured on Government account; and all gains arising therefrom are realized by the Public Treasury.

Prior to the passage of the Coinage Act of 1873, the funds arising from the gain on the minor coinage were available by law for defraying the expenses of the manufacture of such coins. The Act last referred to requires the same to be "covered into the Treasury" without deduction, except for the cost of metals used and the expense of distributing the coins.

The charge for coining gold was finally abrogated under the Act of January 14, 1875, for the resumption of specie payments. The depositor, however, pays for the copper used in alloying his gold.

The charge for coining trade-dollars is required— Coinage Act, 1873—to be fixed from time to time by the Director of the Mint, with the approval of the Secretary of the Treasury, so as to equal but not exceed the average actual cost of coinage at each Mint. The charge for making this coin at the Philadelphia Mint is one and one-fourth per cent., and at the San Francisco and Carson Mints, one and one-half per cent. on the nominal value. This charge covers also the expense of the copper used for alloy.

CHAPTER IX.

COINAGE ACT OF 1873, CHANGE FROM THE STANDARD OF GOLD AND SILVER TO THE GOLD STANDARD.

THE Mint of the United States was originally established at Philadelphia, as that city was at the time—1792—the seat of the National Government. When, a few years afterwards, the seat of government was removed to Washington City, the Mint, because a manufactory, continued at Philadelphia.

In the early years of the Mint, its organization was almost entirely independent of the Treasury Department, and its reports were made direct to the President of the United States. But the legislation in relation to Mints and Coinage, for some years prior to 1870, virtually made the Mint and its branches a Bureau of the Treasury Department. There were, however, provisions of law, conflicting in their character, as to the relative powers and duties of the Secretary of the Treasury and the Director of the Mint. To remedy this, and to consolidate coinage enactments, were the chief objects of the Act, approved Feb. 12, 1873, revising and amending the laws relative to the Mints, Assay-offices, and Coinage of the United States. This Act established the Mint as a Bureau of the Treasury Department, with a chief officer denominated the Director of the Mint, who, under the general direction of the Secretary of the Treasury, has the supervision of all the Mints and Assay-offices of the United States.

The same Act placed the different Mints upon an equality, and devolved the local management of each upon an officer styled the Superintendent; the title of Branch Mint, previously existing as to all the Mints except that at Philadelphia, being changed to that of Mint.

The Act made no change in the standard fineness of any of the coins nor in their standard weight, except that the coining rate of silver into coins of less denomination than the dollar was increased from 384 to $385\frac{8}{10}$ grains (or 25 grams, metric system) to the dollar, which slight increase in weight was made for the purpose of bringing those coins into conformity, as to content of silver, with the five-franc coin of the Latin Union, and the money units of several states in Central and South America. Under the provisions of this Act, the coinage and issue was discontinued, of the silver dollar of $412\tfrac{1}{2}$ grains, the three-cent silver piece, the five-cent silver piece, and the two-cent bronze piece.

Authority was given for the striking, for commercial purposes, of a new coin, denominated the "Trade Dollar," of 420 grains troy (.900 fine,) standard silver. The Act further declared that the one-dollar gold piece, at the standard weight of $25\tfrac{8}{10}$ grains, should be the unit of value, and continued all the gold coins an unlimited tender at their nominal values, when not below the standard and limits of tolerance provided for the single piece; and when reduced in weight below said standard and tolerance, a tender at a valuation in proportion to their actual weight.

It further provided that the gold coins of the United States, if reduced in weight by natural abrasion not more than one-half of one per centum below the standard weight prescribed by law, after a circulation of twenty years as shown by the date of coinage, and at a ratable proportion for any period less than twenty years, should be received at their nominal values by the United States Treasury and its offices, under regulations to be prescribed by the Secretary of the Treasury for the protection of the Government against fraudulent abrasion or other practices.

Previous to the enactment of this law, the double standard of gold and silver had been uninterruptedly in legal existence; although the full legal-tender coins of the two metals had not, for any considerable time, circulated concurrently.

The relative valuation of gold and silver—1 to 15—in the coinage, as established in 1792, continued until 1834, when it was changed to 1 to $15\frac{988}{1000}$, say, one to sixteen nearly, by a reduction in the weight and fineness of the gold coins.

For more than twenty years before this change was made, gold had a higher value in the market than in the nominal or legal-tender value of United States coins; the gold coins, therefore, commanded a premium in the silver coins, and were largely melted or exported.

After the change of standard the silver coins were worth more as bullion than their legal-tender or nominal value, and afterwards gradually disappeared from circulation. To meet this last difficulty, Congress, in 1853, reduced the weight of the silver coins, except the dollar piece, sufficiently to retain them in circulation. The double standard, however, was nominally continued, silver being represented by the dollar piece. This dollar piece, however, was not coined or used as money to any considerable extent on account of its having a higher bullion than nominal or tale value.

The declaration in the Coinage Act of 1873, that the gold dollar was to be thereafter the unit of value, and the omission of the silver dollar from the coins to be struck under the provisions of that Act, placed the United States upon the single gold standard. The silver dollar had already become obsolete in fact; the law of 1873 merely conformed to that fact. This legislation was a continuation and consummation of that which took place in 1834 and 1853, which had for their object the use of gold as the principal money of coin payments in this country.

In respect to this last legislation, it may be said that, at the time it took place and for some time previously, the weight of opinion in Europe and America was against the practicability of maintaining a double standard on any basis which might be selected, and in favor of a single gold standard. This important feature of the Coinage Act of 1873 had been agreed upon by Congress, before it became apparent that a serious decline in the value of silver was likely to take place, in consequence of the change from the silver to the gold standard by the German Empire; and this change in reality could have had no influence in determining the question.

After the great decline in the price of silver had commenced, it was claimed that the discontinuance of the silver dollar had been determined upon without due consideration, especially in view of the large amount of public and private indebtedness.

Whatever difference of opinion may now exist as to the wisdom of the measure, it may be asserted, without the fear of successful contradiction, that no one who favored this legislation had the least idea of giving creditors any advantage over debtors.

Opinions will of course differ as to the propriety of changing the metallic money standard at a time when the actual circulating medium of the country was an irredeemable paper currency, but it is certain that if the legislation, of which complaint is now made, had not occurred, the interest-bearing obligations of the United States would, in the mean time, have depreciated proportionally with the decline in the value of silver; and all attempts to fund obligations at lower rates of interest would no doubt have failed, as it would have been impossible, during the last four years, to have sold at par in gold, public securities legally payable in silver dollars of $412\frac{1}{2}$ grains, United States standard.

Coinage of Twenty-cent Piece of Silver Authorized.

The Act of March 3, 1875, authorized the coinage and issue of a silver piece of the denomination of twenty cents, weighing five grams of standard silver ($77\frac{16}{100}$

grains troy) and a legal tender at its nominal value for any amount not exceeding five dollars in any one payment.

This coin is so near the size of the quarter-dollar that they are not readily distinguishable, and consequently only a limited amount has been coined. It is a convenient decimal division of the dollar, and should have been originally authorized in place of the quarter-dollar piece.

CHAPTER X.

THE TRADE DOLLAR.

THE following extract from a Report made by the author to the Secretary of the Treasury, November 19, 1872, at which time the Coinage Act of 1873 was pending in Congress, shows the grounds on which the coinage of the trade dollar was authorized by that Act.

"*Production of Silver, and Market for the Same.*

"The amount of silver bullion annually produced from the mines of the United States has been increasing during the last three years, and now amounts to about twenty millions per annum, exclusive of the gold it contains; and a further increase in this product being quite certain, the future value of silver as compared with gold is a matter of national importance.

"The fluctuations in the relative value of gold and

silver during the last hundred years have not been very great, but several causes are now at work, all tending to an excess of supply over demand for silver, and its consequent depreciation. Among these causes may be stated the increasing production, its demonetization by the German Empire, and continued disuse in this country, except to a limited extent, as a part of the circulating medium.

"It has also been demonetized by Japan, while in some other countries silver coin has been wholly or partially expelled from circulation by paper money, the effect of which will be to bring to market as bullion large amounts hitherto used as coin. The amount of silver coin in the German Empire at the date of the enactment of the recent coinage law, (December, 1871,) which changed the standard from silver to gold, is estimated by competent authority at $350,000,000, being equal to five years' total production of the globe.

"Even if silver should be adopted by Germany, for subsidiary coinage, not more than $50,000,000 will be required for that purpose, which will leave $300,000,000, or about 9,000 tons, to be disposed of as bullion. A market for this immense supply of silver can only be found in such of the European states as maintain the single standard of silver, or the double standard of gold and silver; and in China and the Indies.

"The facts above stated indicate the gradual but eventually certain adoption of the gold standard, and consequent demonetization of silver by all commercial countries. Not only is the tendency to adopt gold as the sole standard and measure of value, but to use paper money redeemable in gold as the bulk of the circulating medium.

"The true policy of this country under these circumstances is to seek a market in China for its silver bullion; and to do this it must be put in form to meet a favorable reception in that empire.

"The United States silver dollar of $412\frac{1}{2}$ grains has never been well received in China, nor amounted to much as a coin of commerce, for the reason that its bullion value is less than that of the old Spanish dollar, and its successor, the Mexican dollar, both of which have played an important part in the commerce of the world. The standard aimed at when the United States silver dollar was first authorized to be issued was the Spanish dollar. The Act of 1792 provided that the *dollar should be of the value of the Spanish milled dollar, as the same was then current in the United States.* The Act also provided that it should contain $371\frac{1}{4}$ grains of pure silver. The content of pure silver should have been within a fraction of $377\frac{1}{4}$ grains. The mistake made in specifying $371\frac{1}{4}$ instead of $377\frac{1}{4}$ grains, was due to an error in determining the quantity of pure silver in the Spanish dollar, the art of assaying being then imperfectly understood in this country. Dr. Rittenhouse, the first Director of the Mint, must have recognized the error, because the earlier issues of the Mint corresponded very closely to the Spanish dollar. His successor, however, caused the standard to be conformed to law, so that the dollar would contain $371\frac{1}{4}$ grains, which proportion of fine silver has never since been altered.

"Had the United States dollar been issued to correspond in content of fine silver to the old Spanish dollar, as was originally intended, it would no doubt long since have become an important agent of commerce.

"The silver dollar being a useless coin, both as respects circulation and commerce, should be abolished, and we should inquire whether some new medium may not be substituted, approximating in general character and value, which will meet certain commercial requirements becoming daily more pressing, without giving rise to any of those perplexing questions or complications resulting from the varying values of the precious metals, under a double standard, and at the same time afford some relief to our mining industries from the serious decline and further apparent depreciation in the value of silver.

"It appears that the successful inauguration of the China steamship line by the Pacific Mail Company, in connection with the oceanic cables, which now nearly encompass the globe, is producing rapid and highly important changes in the course of exchange.

"From the great advantages in rates and time, the vast business of Europe with China and Japan, which was formerly done by *direct remittances*, is now transacted to a large extent by a *cross exchange* through San Francisco, and will undoubtedly increase as her advantages for arbitrating such exchanges shall become better known.

"For a long time much of the business both of Europe and this country with China and Japan has been done in Mexican dollars, (formerly the Spanish dollar). Indeed this coin has now practically become the money of account in those countries and of commerce with foreign nations, and so necessary has it become for this purpose that it readily commands about 8 per cent. premium both in London and San Francisco, *though intrinsically* worth only $1\frac{6}{10}$ per cent. more than our dollar of $412\frac{1}{2}$ grains.

"This is a serious tax upon our commerce, while our own silver is being exported from the country at a *heavy discount*, and to the serious detriment of both our commerce and mining interests.

"The Japanese are a highly progressive people,

and readily adopt the usages and customs of other nations. They have already adopted a gold standard, and the exchanges with them will be hereafter principally transacted in this metal. The opposition of the Chinese, however, to all innovations is well known, but the magnitude of our present commerce and increasing intercourse with them, together with the inadequate and decreasing supply of Mexican dollars, are rapidly producing a condition of things highly favorable to the introduction of our own dollar, or some other corresponding medium of exchange.

"After consulting with some of the leading business men of San Francisco, as will as with some of the most prominent and intelligent Chinese merchants as to its probable success, I do not hesitate to recommend, in lieu of our old dollar, a new coin or disk, which shall be slightly more valuable than the Mexican dollar, to be made only upon the request of the owner of the bullion, and to be paid for by him.

"It is not proposed to make the new coin or disk a legal tender in payment of debt, but simply a stamped ingot with its weight and fineness indicated. Its manufacture can therefore in no wise give rise to any complication with our monetary system, and neither in theory or principle differ in any respect from the manufacture of unparted or refined bars now authorized by law, except in being of *uniform* weight and fineness.

"If this new coin should be accepted at all as a medium in our trade with China, it will doubtless very soon supersede the Mexican dollar, and there is no reason why it should not in a short time command a premium of 6 or 8 per cent.

"As the product of our silver mines is at present being exported abroad at an average discount of at least 2 per cent., it will be seen at once that such a result would be of immense advantage, not only to our commerce, but also to our mining industries. As this new coin would also be a most desirable form for use in the arts, it would most probably put a stop to the melting of our subsidiary silver coins, now so extensively carried on by silversmiths in certain localities.

"As the trade of San Francisco with China direct, and by exchange for account of the eastern cities and Europe, would readily cover our entire production of silver, it will be seen that a safe outlet for this commodity would be thus secured, and the perplexing proposition as to the decline in price of this metal, and its increasing production, be at once solved in a most satisfactory manner.

"The proposed coin or disk should weigh 420 grains, and contain 378 grains of pure silver, and the weight and fineness be stamped on the reverse of the coin.

"There is certainly sufficient inducement to issue such a coin, and the proposition does not appear to be open to any objection. It will not be a coin of circulation, or legal tender in payment of debts, but simply an agent in our commerce with foreign countries.

"*Comparison of Values.*"

"The Mexican dollar exceeds in value both the Japanese yen and the United States dollar, as will be seen by the following statement:

	WEIGHT.	FINENESS.	PURE SILVER.
Mexican dollar	$417\frac{15}{17}$ grs. troy.	$902\frac{7}{9}$	$377\frac{1}{4}$ grs. troy.
Japanese yen	416 grs. troy.	900	$374\frac{4}{10}$ grs. troy.
American dollar	$412\frac{1}{2}$ grs. troy.	900	$371\frac{1}{4}$ grs. troy.
Proposed new coin	420 grs. troy.	900	378 grs. troy.

"The value of these coins and the proposed commercial dollar may be stated as follows:

United States dollar	$1.00
Japanese yen	$1.00\frac{85}{100}$
Mexican dollar	$1.01\frac{61}{100}$
Proposed new coin	$1.01\frac{88}{100}$

or, say, about $2\frac{7}{10}$ mills more valuable than the Mexican dollar.

"In the event of the issue of the proposed coin it

will be well to give it a title, as for instance "silver union," differing from the coins representing our subsidiary and dollar of account.

Intrinsic value of Mexican dollar as to gold is as	$16\frac{4}{10}$ to 1
At 8 per cent. premium its market price is as	$15\frac{94}{100}$ to 1
American dollar	$15\frac{88}{100}$ to 1
Fine silver at $1\frac{1}{4}$ per cent. premium, San Francisco market rate	$15\frac{79}{100}$ to 1
In London, fine silver at 60d. per (present market rate) standard ounce is	$15\frac{71}{100}$ to 1
Yen of Japan	$16\frac{04}{100}$ to 1
Proposed silver union	$16\frac{28}{100}$ to 1
Five franc, by law	$15\frac{1}{2}$ to 1

"The average price of standard silver in London in 1853 was $61\frac{5}{8}$ pence. The present price is 60 pence per ounce; being a decline of $1\frac{5}{8}$ pence, or $2\frac{3}{4}$ per centum.

"The price of bar-silver, (Doré silver, containing gold,) five years ago, was from 1 to $1\frac{1}{2}$ per cent. premium in San Francisco. The present price of the same is from $1\frac{1}{4}$ to $1\frac{1}{2}$ per cent. discount, being a decline of about $2\frac{1}{2}$ per cent.

"While the average decline in silver in the last twenty years has been about $2\frac{1}{2}$ per cent., the increased weight of the proposed coin, as compared with the silver dollar, is only $1\frac{7}{8}$ per cent."

From the commencement of the coinage of trade dollars, July, 1873, to the close of the fiscal year,

June 30, 1877, 24,581,350 pieces have been struck, nearly all of which have been exported to China.

As a general rule, a better return for silver has been realized when exported to China in the form of trade dollars than in fine bars, notwithstanding the expense of coinage is more than one per cent. above the cost of manufacturing and stamping fine bars; the charge in both cases being paid by the depositor.

This coin is not a legal tender, nor receivable by law in the payment of debts, public or private, and can in no way interfere with our money circulation or money standard.* It is simply in the nature of an ingot, with its weight and fineness certified by the stamp of the United States Mint. At some of the Chinese ports it has been made by the proper authorities a legal tender, and as such is used as a dollar in money transactions the same as the Mexican dollar.

The trade dollar possesses decided advantages over the other dollars with which the Chinese are familiar, by reason of its superior mintage and its more accurate conformity to standard weight and fineness; and it will, no doubt, continue to increase in favor in China, as no coinage of gold or silver is executed in that empire.

---

* When the coinage of the trade dollar was first authorized, it was inadvertently made a legal tender to the amount of five dollars. Section 2, Act of July 22, 1876, repealed its legal-tender character altogether.

The following reports made by the two leading foreign banks of China, the Oriental Bank, and the Hong Kong and Shanghai Banking Corporation, dated, respectively, January 31 and 30, 1877, and furnished by the United States Consulate at Hong Kong to the Secretary of the Treasury, show to what extent the trade dollar has gained a footing in China, and the estimation with which it is regarded by the Chinese.

"The United States trade dollar has been well received in China and is eagerly welcomed in those parts of the country where the true value of the coin is known. It is a legal tender at the ports Foochow and Canton in China, and also at Saigon and Singapore, and although not legally current in this colony, it is anxiously sought after by the Chinese, and in the bazaars it is seldom to be purchased. In proof of the estimation in which the trade dollar is held in the South of China, we need only state that the bulk of the direct exchange business between San Francisco and Hong Kong (which is very considerable) is done in this coin, the natives preferring it to the Mexican dollar. Late advices from San Francisco report that so great is the demand for trade dollars for shipment to China that the California Mint is unequal to the task of turning out the coin fast enough to satisfy requirements. This is, in our estimation, evidence powerful enough to convince the most skeptical as to whether the United States trade dollar has been a success or not. 'It is the best dollar we have ever seen here, and as there can be no doubt as to the standard and purity being maintained, it will become more popular day by day, and, we doubt not, ultimately find its way into the North of China, where the people are more prejudiced against innovation."

"Trade dollars are current by count at Singapore, Penang, Bangkok and Saigon; they are current by weight at Swatow, Amoy, Foochow and Canton. In Hong Kong they are not a legal tender, and the banks will only take them from each other by special arrangement; but the Chinese take them freely in Hong Kong when they want coin of any description, which is very seldom, as they prefer bank notes, and only take coin from the banks when they require to export it from the colony. In the South of China, the Straits and Cochin China, the trade dollar is well known, and passes without comment along with the clean Mexican dollars, but in Shanghai, and the northern ports, it is unknown, and is not likely to be current for a length of time.

"My opinion is that ultimately it will be current all over China; it is the best coin that ever has been imported, and being produced at the fountain-head of silver, can be laid down more cheaply than any other dollar. The reliable character of the coin (for weight or purity) is a further consideration, which must be favorably entertained.

"China requires many millions of dollars annually, and while the clean Mexican dollar will be imported for the North of China, the trade dollar will be imported for the South. I would roughly estimate that the San Francisco steamers will bring from four to six lacs* of trade dollars each fortnightly trip, all the year round. I base this estimate upon the experience of last season's requirements."

The United States now produces, and will no doubt produce for many years to come, more silver than any other country. This production will probably be in excess of the requirements for the coinage of circulating money. We shall therefore continue to be exporters of that metal, and it is important that it should be put in the form best calculated to meet with favor in other countries. As the trade dollar has been so well received in one of the great empires of the globe where silver is so largely used, its coinage should be provided for to the extent which may be required.

*Four to six hundred thousand.

CHAPTER XI.

GOLD IN THE FORM OF MINT BARS, AUTHORIZED TO BE HELD AND EXCHANGED BY THE ASSISTANT TREASURER AT NEW YORK.

THE Act of January 22, 1874, provides:

"That the Secretary of the Treasury may, from time to time, transfer to the office of the Assistant Treasurer at New York, from the bullion fund of the Assay-office at New York, refined gold bars bearing the United States stamp of fineness, weight and value, or bars from any melt of foreign gold coin or bullion of standard equal to or above that of the United States, and may apply the same to the redemption of coin certificates, or in exchange for gold coin at par, and not less than the market value, subject to such regulations as he may prescribe."

It is a well known fact that in exporting specie, newly coined and full-weighted pieces are selected for that purpose.

The effect of such a discrimination is, of course, to

send out of the country the perfect coins and leave worn pieces at home.

The intention of Congress in passing an Act authorizing the Treasury to hold mint bars for exchange was, no doubt, to encourage shipment in that form instead of coin; and this has become of some importance since the coinage charge was repealed.

Fine gold bars, when they are in demand for manufacturing purposes, or when foreign exchange is at the shipping point, generally command a premium of one-eighth per cent.

The keeping in the Treasury of a fund in the form of mint bars to take the place of coin at times when the export of specie becomes unavoidable, will prove an important matter on and after the resumption of specie payments.

The gold bars are stamped as to value at the coining rate or mint price of gold in the United States,— $23\frac{22}{100}$ grains of pure gold to the dollar, or $25\frac{8}{10}$ grains United States standard of nine parts fine and one alloy.

CHAPTER XII.

COINAGE FOR FOREIGN STATES AT THE MINTS OF THE UNITED STATES.

THE following Act was approved Jan. 29, 1874: "That it shall be lawful for coinage to be executed at the Mints of the United States for any foreign country applying for the same, according to the legally prescribed standards and devices of such country, under such regulations as the Secretary of the Treasury may prescribe; and the charge for the same shall be equal to the expenses thereof, including labor, materials, and use of machinery, to be fixed by the Director of the Mint with the approval of the Secretary of the Treasury; *provided* that the manufacture of such coin shall not interfere with the regular coinage of the United States."

The monetary unit of most of the Central and South American Governments is a silver dollar, corresponding in content of fine silver with two United States half-dollar pieces or other coined divisions comprising a dollar in value.

Our silver coins of less denomination than the dollar have been exported to some extent, since 1853, to Central and South America, where they circulate as money, and whence they may be expected to return to us in a worn condition, to be re-coined at the expense of the United States. The intention of Congress in passing the foregoing Act was, no doubt, to prevent the export of change-money, as well as to promote commerce with certain countries having no mints of their own.

CHAPTER XIII.

LEGAL TENDER.

Legal Tender of the Gold, Silver, and Minor Coins of the United States, and United States Notes, as prescribed in the Revised Statutes of the United States, 1874.

THE following extracts from the Statutes are given for the purpose of showing what constitutes *legal tender* in the United States. The only change made since the revision of the Statutes is the repeal of the legal-tender quality of the trade dollar.

SEC. 3584. No foreign gold or silver coins shall be a legal tender in payment of debts.

SEC. 3585. The gold coins of the United States shall be a legal tender in all payments at their nominal value, when not below the standard weight and limit of tolerance provided by law for the single piece, and, when reduced in weight below such standard and tolerance, shall be a legal tender at a valuation in proportion to their actual weight.

Sec. 3586. The silver coins of the United States shall be a legal tender, at their nominal value, for any amount not exceeding five dollars in any one payment.

Sec. 3587. The minor coins of the United States shall be a legal tender, at their nominal value, for any amount not exceeding twenty-five cents in any one payment.

Sec. 3588. United States notes shall be lawful money, and a legal tender in payment of all debts, public and private, within the United States, except for duties on imports and interest on the public debt.

Sec. 3589. Demand Treasury notes authorized by the Act of July 17, 1861, chapter 5, and the Act of February 12, 1862, chapter 20, shall be lawful money and a legal tender in like manner as United States notes.

Sec. 3590. Treasury notes issued under the authority of the Acts of March 3, 1863, chapter 73, and June 30, 1864, chapter 172, shall be legal tender to the same extent as United States notes for their face value, excluding interest: *Provided*, that Treasury notes issued under the Act last named shall not be a legal tender in payment or redemption of any notes issued by any bank, banking association, or banker, calculated and intended to circulate as money.

CHAPTER XIV.

PAR OF EXCHANGE AND VALUE OF FOREIGN COINS.

THE true or mint par of exchange, between two countries, is the exact equivalent of the standard money of one country correctly expressed in the money terms of the other; the basis of comparison being the quantity of pure metal declared by law to represent the unit of their moneys of account, respectively.

As it is upon this basis that trade between nations is conducted, international debts discharged, and remittances from one country to another made, it is important that the true or mint par, and not a technical par, should prevail. A technical par of exchange between Great Britain and the United States prevailed prior to Jan. 1, 1874. It had its origin in colonial times, and was based on a comparison of the pound sterling, represented at the time by silver, with the Spanish dollar of 386 grains of fine silver.

This technical par became, of late years, objectionable in many respects, and, together with the undervaluation of different foreign moneys by various Acts of Congress, finally became the subject of discussion. The attention of the Secretary of the Treasury was first called to the defective system by the author in his Report of Nov. 19, 1872, as follows:

"*Valuation of Foreign Coins.*

"The correct valuation of foreign coins is a subject which should receive consideration in connection with the revision of the coinage laws, and I venture to suggest for reasons herein stated, that provision be made by law to the effect that, in all customs transactions, the pound sterling, and other foreign gold coins, be computed and stated according to the intrinsic value in our money of account of the fine gold contained.

"The importance of this subject will be seen by reference to the existing mode of computing and adjusting exchanges between the United States and Great Britain. The sovereign, which represents the pound sterling, contains 113.0016+ grains pure gold, and is of the value of 4.86\frac{6.5}{100}$ in our money of account; but this is not the value at which it is computed in settlement of accounts between the two countries, and in estimating, at the custom-houses, the duties to be paid on imports. In both cases it is undervalued more than two cents.

"This undervaluation of the sovereign entails a loss, not only on the American exporter, but on the Government.. If the exporter has £20,000 placed to his credit in London, he has there the equivalent of $97,330—each pound containing $4.86\frac{65}{100}$, and assuming exchange on London to be at par, he ought to receive the sum stated.

"But such is not the case: as, when he makes a draft against the sum to his credit, he must, in accordance with commercial custom, compute the pound sterling at $4.84\frac{4}{10}$, and consequently receive only $96,880, subjecting himself to a loss of $450 on the transaction.

"The banker, however, who cashes his draft remits it as cover to his own exchange, and receives the full pound in London.

"In the other case, an invoice of British merchandise amounting to £20,000, and subject to duty, being received, is converted into United States money, at the rate of $4.84\frac{4}{10}$ to the pound sterling (instead of $4.86\frac{65}{100}$), and the duty levied on $96.880 instead of $97.330.

"The valuation of the pound sterling at $4.84\frac{4}{10}$ instead of $4.86\frac{65}{100}$ may be claimed to be proper, in view of the fact that to actually convert a sovereign into United States coin entails a deduction of nearly 2½ cents in consequence of the one-half per cent. coinage charge. If the United States coinage charge be the real cause of the undervaluation of the pound sterling, no time should be lost in abrogating it, our commerce and monetary transactions with Great Britain being too extensive to admit of such a disadvantage.

"With proper legislation the disadvantage referred to would be removed, and the complicated mode of computing exchange with Great Britain be simplified. The par of the pound sterling would be 4.86\frac{65}{100}$, and would be quoted at that rate. . . .

"The present fictitious par of exchange is arrived at by adding 9 per cent. to the old custom-house valuation of $4.44.4 for the pound sterling, and when exchange is at par it is quoted at 109. This complicated system also leads to a fictitious quotation of our bonds in the London market, which, when at par, are quoted at a deduction corresponding to the percentage added here to the old valuation above referred to.

"That a system so fictitious as this should have been adhered to for nearly a century after the coins and their content of fine metal on which it was originally based have passed away, shows the tenacity with which mankind adhere to monetary terms and customs.

"The following section is respectfully suggested:

"'That in converting invoices of foreign merchandise received at the several custom-houses, and subject to duty, into United States money of account, the monetary unit in which such invoices are stated shall be estimated at the intrinsic value of the fine gold contained in the coins representing such units respectively, and it shall be the duty of the Director of the Mint to cause assays to be made annually of such foreign coins as are known to our commerce, and present a statement thereof in his annual report.'

"The following extracts from the report made by Senator Sherman, in 1868, on the subject of international coinage, strongly present the disadvantage under which we labor in connection with our foreign exchanges:

"'Every advance toward a free exchange of commodities is an advance in civilization. . . . Every obstruction to commerce is a tax upon consumption; every facility to a free exchange cheapens commodities, increases trade and production, and promotes civilization. . . . No single measure will tend in this direction more than the adoption of a fixed international standard of value by which all products may be measured, and in conformity with which the coin of a country may go with its flag into every sea and buy the products of every nation without being discounted by the money-changer.

. . . .

"'Gold with us is like cotton—a raw product. . . . Every obstruction to its free use, such as the necessity of its re-coinage when passing from nation to nation, diminishes its value, and that loss falls on the United States, the country of production.

. . . .

"'The United States is a new nation, and therefore a debtor nation. By placing ourselves in harmony with the money units of creditor nations we promote the easy borrowing of money and payment of debts without the loss of re-coinage or exchange, always paid by the debtor. . . .

"'The technical rate of exchange between the United States and Great Britain, growing out of the different nominal values of coin, is a standing reproach which can only be got rid of by unifying the coinage of the two countries, when both the real and technical rates of exchange will be at par, etc.'"

The subject was considered by the Finance Committee of the Senate at the next session of Congress, and on March 3, 1873, the following Act, establishing a new rule for the valuation of foreign coins and fixing the par of exchange between the

United States and Great Britain, was passed, and took effect January 1, 1874.

"*An Act to establish the Custom-House value of the sovereign or pound sterling of Great Britain, and to fix the par of exchange.*

"Be it enacted, by the Senate and House of Representatives of the United States of America in Congress assembled, that the value of foreign coin as expressed in the money of account of the United States shall be that of the pure metal of such coin of standard value; and the values of the standard coins in circulation of the various nations of the world shall be estimated annually by the Director of the Mint, and be proclaimed on the first day of January by the Secretary of the Treasury.

"SEC. 2. That in all payments by or to the Treasury, whether made here or in foreign countries, where it becomes necessary to compute the value of the sovereign or pound sterling, it shall be deemed equal to four dollars eighty-six cents and six and one-half mills, and the same rule shall be applied in appraising merchandise imported, where the value is, by the invoice, in sovereigns or pounds sterling, and in the construction of contracts payable in sovereigns or pounds sterling, and this valuation shall be the par of exchange between Great Britain and the

United States; and all contracts made after the first day of January, eighteen hundred and seventy-four, based on an assumed par of exchange with Great Britain of fifty-four pence to the dollar, or four dollars forty-four and four-ninths cents to the sovereign or pound sterling, shall be null and void.

"SEC. 3. That all Acts and parts of Acts inconsistent with these provisions be and the same are hereby repealed."

In converting invoices of foreign merchandise, stated in foreign moneys of account, into the money of account of the United States, it was necessary to make such conversion according to values ascertained under the rule laid down in the 1st section of the law.

The employment at the Custom-Houses of the values thus ascertained led to some dissatisfaction, the duties being increased, not in proportion to the slightly enhanced values of the coins, but under the operation of an artificial rule in laying duties.

Appeals in certain cases were taken, one of which, involving the value of the franc, was made a test case on which the construction given the law by the Treasury Department was sustained by the decision of the United States Supreme Court.

The important and useful reform which this Act brought about in respect to the par of exchange between the United States and Great Britain, has not been attended by any difficulty, nor has there been a single case of litigation in connection with the same.

The valuation of foreign coins under former laws was based upon the assay of actual pieces, many of which were more or less reduced in weight from the attrition of circulation, and therefore were not standard coins.

Under the new Act the value of foreign moneys, expressed in our money of account, is determined by comparing the pure gold which the law of any country declares to represent its money unit, with the pure gold contained in the standard gold dollar of the United States; in other words, we have an exact comparison of money standards instead of individual coins in circulation.

The value in our money terms of the money units of the various nations of the world, determined under the requirements of the new law, are as follows:

4

MONEY AND LEGAL TENDER.

Country.	Monetary unit.	Standard.	Value in U.S. money.	Standard coin.
Austria	Florin	Silver	.45,3	Florin.
Belgium	Franc	Gold and silver	.19,3	5, 10, and 20 francs.
Bolivia	Dollar	Gold and silver	.96,5	Escudo, ½ bolivar and bolivar.
Brazil	Milreis of 1,000 reis	Gold	.54,5	None.
British Possessions in North America	Dollar	Gold	$1.00	
Bogota	Peso	Gold	.96,5	Dollar.
Central America	Dollar	Silver	.91,8	Condor, doubloon, and escudo.
Chili	Peso	Gold	.91,2	10 and 20 crowns.
Denmark	Crown	Gold	.26,8	Dollar.
Ecuador	Dollar	Silver	.91,8	
Egypt	Pound of 100 piasters	Gold	4.97,4	5, 10, 25, and 50 piasters.
France	Franc	Gold and silver	.19,3	5, 10, and 20 francs.
Great Britain	Pound sterling	Gold	4.86,6½	½ sovereign and sovereign.
Greece	Drachma	Gold and silver	.19,3	5, 10, 20, 50, and 100 drachmas.
German Empire	Mark	Gold	.23,8	5, 10, and 20 marks.
Japan	Yen	Gold	.99,7	1, 2, 5, 10, and 20 yen.
India	Rupee of 16 annas	Silver	.43,6	
Italy	Lira	Gold and silver	.19,3	5, 10, 20, 50, and 100 lire.
Liberia	Dollar	Gold	1.00	
Mexico	Dollar	Silver	.99,8	Peso or dollar, 5, 10, 25, and 50 centavo.
Netherlands	Florin	Gold and silver	.38,5	Florin; ten guldens, gold, ($4.01,9.)
Norway	Crown	Gold	.26,8	10 and 20 crowns.
Peru	Dollar	Silver	.91,8	
Portugal	Milreis of 1,000 reis	Gold	1.08	2, 5, and 10 milreis.
Russia	Rouble of 100 copecks	Silver	.73,4	¼, ½, and 1 rouble.
Sandwich Islands	Dollar	Gold	1.00	
Spain	Peseta of 100 centimes	Gold and silver	.19,3	5, 10, 20, 50, and 100 pesetas.
Sweden	Crown	Gold	.26,8	10 and 20 crowns.
Switzerland	Franc	Gold and silver	.19,3	5, 10, and 20 francs
Tripoli	Mahbub of 20 piasters	Silver	.82,9	
Tunis	Piaster of 16 caroubs	Silver	.11,8	
Turkey	Piaster	Gold	.04,3	
United States of Colombia	Peso	Silver	.91,8	25, 50, 100, 250, and 500 piasters.

In the foregoing table gold is valued and computed at the rate of $23\frac{22}{100}$ grains of fine gold to the dollar. The silver units are calculated according to the United States trade dollar valuation, or 378 grains of fine silver to the dollar.

CHAPTER XV.

PAPER CURRENCY SINCE 1862.

Issue of Legal-Tender notes on the credit of the United States.

ONE of the most important measures in relation to money ever taken in this country, was the enactment of the law of February 25, 1862, authorizing the issue of United States notes on the credit of the Government, and making the same a legal tender without limit, in the payment of debts, public and private, except duties on imports and interest on United States bonds.

This was peculiarly and exclusively a war measure, and should never be regarded as a precedent to be followed under any circumstances in time of peace, or even of ordinary war.

These notes, in consequence of the large sums from time to time issued, and the increasing magnitude of the civil war then prevailing, began speedily to depreciate in value as compared with gold and silver. They soon became, and have since continued to be, practically, the actual money of the country. When their issue commenced the metallic money standard was as follows:

All gold coins of the United States were a legal tender at their nominal value and without limit.

Silver dollars coined by the same authority were in like manner a legal tender, and the Mints were open for such coinage to any one who might choose to deposit bullion for the same.

The silver coins of less denomination than the dollar piece (except the three-cent pieces) were a legal tender in any sum not exceeding five dollars.

When the issue of legal-tender notes commenced, all private money obligations became dischargeable in such notes, except those which, by their terms, were payable in coin only.

The term "coin" in the Act authorizing the issue of these notes, referred to United States coin of full legal-tender quality, *i. e.*, gold coins and the silver dollar. It also embraced silver coins of less denomination than the dollar, except the three-cent piece coined prior to 1853.

It was of course well known at the time of the enactment of the law, that the silver coins of less denomination than the dollar, coined prior to the year

1853, had nearly all been re-coined, and that the silver dollar had, for some years previous, ceased to be coined to any extent, and this for the reason that its bullion value exceeded its nominal or tale value, or in other words $412\frac{1}{2}$ grains of standard silver were worth from $1\frac{1}{2}$ to 3 per cent. more in the market, in our gold coin, than a gold dollar. The double standard, nevertheless, had a legal existence, while thus practically obsolete.

CHAPTER XVI.

ISSUE OF FRACTIONAL NOTES.

SOON after the issue of United States notes commenced, gold and silver coin commanded a premium in such notes, and virtually ceased to circulate, except in the states of California and Nevada, where the metallic standard was adhered to, and where it has since been maintained to the exclusion of paper money.

The inconvenience caused by the withdrawal of the silver coin from circulation was at first met by the issue of postage and revenue stamps, and fractional notes commonly called postal currency.

The 4th Section of the Act of March 3, 1863, entitled "An Act to provide ways and means for the support of the Government," authorized the Secretary of the Treasury to issue, in lieu of the foregoing, fractional notes of like amounts, in such form as he might deem expedient, all such notes issued to be exchangeable, by the Assistant Treasurers and designated depositaries, for United States notes, in sums not less than three dollars, and to be receivable for postage and revenue stamps, and also in payment of any dues to the government less than five dollars, except duties on imports, and to be redeemed on presentation at the Treasury of the United States in such sums, and under such regulations, as the Secretary of the Treasury should prescribe. The issue of this fractional currency, including postage and revenue stamps issued as currency, was limited to $50,000,000.

These fractional notes constituted the change-money until April 20, 1876, when, under the provisions of the Act of January 14, 1875, for the resumption of specie payments, and the Act of April 17, 1876, providing for the issue of silver coin in place of fractional currency, their redemption commenced and has since continued, silver coin of less denomination than the dollar being issued in their place.

CHAPTER XVII.

COIN CERTIFICATES.

THE 5th section of the Act of March 3, 1863, authorized the Secretary of the Treasury to receive deposits of gold coin and bullion at the offices of the United States Treasurer and Assistant Treasurers, in sums not less than twenty dollars, and to issue certificates therefor in denominations of not less than twenty dollars each, corresponding with the denominations of the United States notes, the coin and bullion deposited for or representing the certificates of deposit to be retained in the Treasury for the payment of the same on demand.

The same section provided that certificates representing coin in the Treasury might be issued in payment of interest on the public debt, which certificates, together with those issued for coin and bullion deposited, should not at any time exceed twenty per centum of the amount of coin and bullion in the Treasury, and that these certificates should be received at par in payment for duties on imports. Under the provisions of this section, coin certificates, redeemable only at the office of the Assistant Treasurer of the United States in the City of New York, have been from time to time issued by the Treasury; but bullion deposits for such notes have not been made.

CHAPTER XVIII

NATIONAL CURRENCY SECURED BY A PLEDGE OF UNITED STATES STOCKS.

ON Feb. 25, 1863, an Act to provide a National Currency, secured by a pledge of United States Bonds, and for the circulation and redemption of such currency, was approved.

The most important features of this Act were:

1. Security to the note holders.

2. The issue and circulation of national bank notes as money.

3. The making of these notes receivable at par, in all parts of the United States, in payments for taxes, excises, public lands, and all other dues to the United States, except duties on imports, and also for all salaries and other debts and demands owing by the United States to individuals, corporations, and associations within the United States, except interest on the public debt.

4. Redemption, or payment of national currency

notes, in lawful money of the United States (gold and silver coin of legal-tender character, and United States legal-tender notes.)

5. Failure to redeem in lawful money is followed by certain proceedings,—sale of the pledged bonds, and redemption of the notes with proceeds thereof, by the United States.

The limits of this work will not permit further reference to this Act, or the various amendments thereto; but it should be added that the system has secured uniformity in the current value of the notes throughout the Union, and consequent saving of expense on domestic exchange, with a perfect security to the holder, and thus far proved greatly superior to any other system of bank issues which has obtained in the United States.

CHAPTER XIX.

LEGISLATION FOR FUNDING AND EVENTUAL PAYMENT OF THE OBLIGATIONS OF THE UNITED STATES IN COIN.

THE Act of February 25, 1862, authorized the issue, on the credit of the United States, of one hundred and fifty million dollars in United States legal-tender notes, and made provision for funding the same, together with the floating debt of the United States, into six per cent. bonds. It also contained the following important features.

That all duties on imported goods should be paid in coin, or in notes payable on demand, and heretofore authorized to be issued, and by law receivable in payment of public dues; and that the coin so paid should be set apart as a special fund to be applied, first, "To the payment in coin of the interest on the bonds and notes of the United States;" second, "To the purchase or payment of one per centum of the entire debt of the United States, to be made within each fiscal year after the first day of July, eighteen hundred and sixty-two, which is to be set apart as a sinking-fund, the interest of which shall in like manner be applied to the purchase or payment of the public debt, as the Secretary of the Treasury shall from time to time direct;" third, "The residue thereof to be paid into the Treasury of the United States."

These provisions of law were made for the purpose of protecting the credit of the United States, then more than ever important, as events clearly indicated that the civil war, which had already commenced, would become one of great magnitude, and necessarily entail expenses on a corresponding scale. To meet these expenses the borrowing, from time to time, of large sums of money would be necessary; and this could be done most readily by surrounding the public credit with every possible safeguard.

Retirement and Cancellation of United States Notes.

The Act of March 12, 1866, authorized the Secretary of the Treasury, at his discretion, to receive any Treasury Notes, or other obligations issued under any Act of Congress, whether bearing interest or not, in exchange for any description of bonds authorized by the Act of March 3, 1865; and also to dispose of any description of bonds, authorized by said Act, either in the United States or elsewhere, to such an amount, in such manner, and at such rates, as he might think advisable, for lawful money of the United States, or for any Treasury Notes, Certificates of Indebtedness, or Certificates of Deposit, or other representatives of value, which had been or might be issued under any Act of Congress; the proceeds thereof to be used only for retiring the Treasury Notes, or other obligations, issued under any Act of Congress.

This Act further provided that of United States Notes not more than ten million of dollars should be retired and canceled within six months from its passage, and that, thereafter, not more than four million dollars, in any one month, should be retired and canceled.

The authority thus given to reduce the legal-tender paper currency, by retirement and cancellation, was suspended by the Act of February 4, 1868, but not until more than seventy-two million dollars in legal-tender notes had been retired, leaving the amount outstanding $356,000,000. The intention of the Act providing for the retirement of United States notes was to bring about an early resumption of specie payment, by contracting the volume of the paper currency.

The change of financial policy, with reference to specie resumption, unsettled, in some degree, the public credit, and various propositions, looking to the payment of the public debt in United States notes, and an indefinite continuation of the credit paper-money system, were advanced. To remove all doubts as to the character of the obligations of the United States, and the intention to pay the same in coin, the following Act was passed March 18, 1869:

"That in order to remove any doubt as to the purpose of the Government to discharge all just obligations to the public creditors, and to settle conflicting questions and interpretations of the laws by virtue of which such obligations have been contracted, it is hereby provided and declared that the faith of the United States is solemnly pledged to the payment in coin, or its equivalent, of all the obligations of the United States, not bearing interest, known as United States notes, and of all the interest-bearing obligations of the United States, except in cases where the law, authorizing the issue of any such obligation, has expressly provided that the same may be paid in lawful money, or other currency than gold and silver. But none of such interest-bearing obligations, not already due, shall be redeemed or paid before maturity, unless at such time United States notes shall be convertible into coin, at the option of the holder, or unless at such time bonds of the United States, bearing a lower rate of interest than the bonds to be redeemed, can be sold at par in coin, and the United States also solemnly pledges its faith to to make provision, at the earliest practicable period, for the redemption of the United States notes in coin."

By this last Act, Congress substantially declared that all notes of the United States were simply credit obligations, and pledged the public faith to their payment in coin of the then existing standard, *i.e.*, gold coins of the United States, $25\frac{8}{10}$ grains, $\frac{9}{10}$ fine, to the dollar, and silver dollar coins, of $412\frac{1}{2}$ grains of the same fineness.

Section six of the Act of June 20, 1874, provided "that the amount of United States notes outstanding, and to be used as a part of the circulating medium, shall not exceed the sum of $382,000,000; and that no part thereof shall be held or used as a reserve." This section of law was no doubt intended to legalize the re-issue of United States notes to the amount of $26,000,000 made by the Treasury Department at, or shortly after, the commencement of the severe financial revulsion which occurred in this country in September, 1873, as well as to prevent the withdrawal of the same, or any part thereof, under the provisions of any law existing at that time. The Act of January 14, 1875, authorized, on certain conditions, the increase of the circulation of National Bank notes without respect to the limit previously existing, and provided that legal-tender notes, to the amount of eighty per centum of the National Bank notes thereafter issued, should be redeemed. This redemption of United States notes was to continue until the outstanding issue should be reduced to $300,000,000, and then cease.

This last act further declares that on and after the first day of January, 1879, the legal-tender notes which may then be outstanding shall be redeemed in coin. It also clothes the Secretary of the Treasury with certain powers for carrying its various provisions into effect. The retirement and cancellation of United States notes, in accordance with the provisions of this act, has since been gradually going on.

This law is silent as to the disposition to be made of United States notes which may be redeemed in coin on and after January 1, 1879. The notes which have been redeemed up to the present time, under the provisions of this Act, have been canceled; but this has been done under the clearly expressed intention to reduce the outstanding issue to $300,000,000. It is probable that the Secretary of the Treasury would have the right to consider the notes which may be redeemed after January 1, 1879, as available money in the Treasury.

If such a construction of the law is not correct, and these notes are to be canceled, serious embarrassments may result, especially if the amount of National Bank notes which may be in circulation, together with the stock of coin at the term fixed for the redemption of United States notes, should prove to be insufficient for the requirements of the country.

It has been urged, as the United States Supreme Court sustained the legal-tender Act only on the plea of necessity, that the designation by Congress of a date, January 1, 1879, when the notes shall be redeemed in coin, is also, by implication, a declaration that the war necessity has ended, and therefore, after that date, the re-issue of these legal-tender notes by the Government cannot be sustained.

CHAPTER XX.

MINT WEIGHTS AND WEIGHING OF BULLION AND COIN.

IN all transactions in the precious metals, either purchase or sale, the fabrication of coins, jewelry and plate, or in exchanges with foreign countries, it is absolutely necessary that some unvarying standard of weight or measure should be adopted for use, and established by law.

In the early days of our Mint, bullion, ingots and coins in bulk, were weighed in pounds, ounces, pennyweights and grains; the pounds being reduced to ounces in entering the account in the Register. Some of these old-style bullion weights of the Mint are still extant. They are bell-shaped, with large handles and screw-plugs for convenience in adjusting. They were made in England and bear various stamps, such as "Royal Mint" with the figure of a crown, "D.C.G." and a crown, etc.; and though without dates they were probably imported at the time of the establishment of our Mint. They were used until 1835–6, when new sets were made, based on the weight of 1827, hereafter described, which is now the standard mint weight. These weights consisted of the troy ounce as the unit, with its multiples and decimal subdivisions,—the troy pound having been practically discarded.

The Standard Troy Pound of England has a well ascertained pedigree of three and a half centuries. There is no recognized weight in England of higher antiquity. It was extant in the time of Henry VIII; but to prevent conflict with another money-pound, it was constituted by that king, in 1526, the standard mint weight, and was lodged in Goldsmiths' Hall. In 1588, Queen Elizabeth directed that a copy of this pound should be deposited at the Exchequer, and another copy at the Mint. In 1758 a committee was appointed in the House of Commons to examine into the discrepancies among existing weights, and prepare a pound that should thereafter be the standard. The "Parliamentary Pound" thus established, prepared by Mr. Bird and Mr. Harris, the Master of the Mint, is carefully kept in custody of the Speaker of the Commons.

An exact duplicate of this pound was procured in 1827 for the use of the mint of the United States, by Albert Gallatin, then our minister at London, and was formally certified by the President of the United States, and afterwards declared to be the standard troy pound weight for the regulation of the coinage, by act of Congress of May 19, 1828.

This weight was made and compared by Mr. Bate and Capt. Kater, well known experts in England, who declared, as the result of the average of various weighings, that the difference between it and the Parliamentary Pound could not be greater than $\frac{1}{800}$ of a grain.

To illustrate the difficulty experienced in obtaining precision in weights, it may be stated that some years since, when the mint was receiving large amounts of silver bullion from the Spanish-American States, it was thought important to have an authentic copy of the Castilian mark; and accordingly one was procured through Mr. Poinsett, our minister to Mexico, and another through Mr. Everett, our minister to Spain. These weights, although they had been made with the utmost care, were found to vary about four grains.

The same difficulty and uncertainty have attached to the *étalons* of the French kilogram, the exact relation of which to troy weight is, however, now settled by law. In practice it will always be difficult to find two kilogram weights precisely equal.

Each Mint and Assay-office of the United States is

provided with a set of accurately adjusted standard weights, by comparison with which the working weights, or those used in the daily transactions of business, are carefully adjusted once a year.

In the weighing of bullion for coinage purposes, fractions less than $\frac{1}{100}$ of an ounce for gold and $\frac{5}{100}$ of an ounce for silver are disregarded.

Gold coins and trade dollars are adjusted by the single piece, and a deviation from the legal weight is not allowed of more than a half grain for the double-eagle and eagle, and of a quarter grain for the half-eagle, three-dollar piece, quarter-eagle and gold dollar. The silver coins must not deviate more than 1½ grains per piece. This deviation is what is known as the *Mint Remedy* or *Tolerance* for weight.

Silver coins of less denomination than the trade dollar are not adjusted by hand, but are brought within the remedy by carefully regulating the thickness of the fillets or strips into which the ingots are rolled and from which the planchets or blanks for the coins are cut. The coinage law requires that in every delivery of gold coin made by the coiner to the superintendent, there shall not be a deviation of more than $\frac{1}{100}$ of an ounce for every \$5000 in double-eagles, eagles, half-eagles, or quarter-eagles, and for every 1000 pieces of the three-dollar or dollar piece; and in silver coins no greater deviation than $\frac{2}{100}$ of an ounce in 1000 trade dollars, half-dollars or quarter-dollars, and $\frac{1}{100}$ of an ounce in 1000 dimes. In making up drafts for delivery it would be difficult always to come within these limits if the coins were taken promiscuously, and therefore in practice the drafts are made up by a judicious admixture of what are technically called "heavies" and "lights," coins slightly heavier or lighter than the true standard weight, yet not enough so to exceed the tolerance.

In ascertaining the value of bullion, it is just as necessary that accuracy should be attained in fixing the fineness as in finding the true weight; and the method of assaying in our Mints and in those of Europe has not only been simplified by the introduction of the metric system of weights, but a far greater degree of accuracy has been thereby attained.

Until about the year 1836, the carat system was used for expressing fineness in our Mint, as well as throughout Europe with the exception of France. It is still much practiced in England, and is in vogue with manufacturers, dealers and purchasers of jewelry, as to gold fineness, everywhere. Fine gold is represented by 24 carats fine, the carat being divided into 4 carat-grains (which do not, however, coincide with troy grains), and the grain into eighths. Formerly the 24 carat weight was not a fixed quantity, though latterly in England it is taken as 12 grains troy, that being a convenient quantity of metal to use for an assay.

The normal weight used at present for the assay of gold is the half-gram of the metric system, equal to 7.716 grains troy. The equivalent weight of the French gramme in grains, was fixed by act of Congress of July 28, 1866, at 15.432 grains troy.

The carat system does not admit of a close expression of fineness. As 24 carats stand for absolute purity, and as the carat is divided into 4 carat-grains, and these into eighths, it is seen that as $24 \times 4 \times 8 = 768$, the lowest expression of fineness is $\frac{1}{768}$ part. Assays by the metric system are now reported to the $\frac{1}{10000}$ part, and its decimal notation also greatly abridges the labor of calculations. The standard fineness of gold coin of the United States, prior to 1834, was 22 carats, the same as the present English and Russian standard, and assays were reported as being so many carats and grains better or worse than this standard; these variations being technically called *betterness* and *worseness*. The present method is to report in thousandths and tenths of thousandths; fine gold being represented by 1000.

The assay weights for silver were on a different basis. The primary or chief weight was called the assay pound, or 12 ounces, which represented absolutely fine silver. This pound was divided into ounces, pennyweights and grains, answerable to the troy scale. The closest report was the half-pennyweight or 12 grains in the pound, *i. e.*, $\frac{12}{5760}$ or $\frac{1}{480}$; while reports by the metric system are now made to $\frac{1}{2000}$ and can be made to $\frac{1}{4000}$.

These complicated and inconvenient methods of expressing fineness were superseded in 1837 by the adoption of the standard of $\frac{900}{1000}$ for both gold and silver, and the employment of a decimal notation at the Mint.

CHAPTER XXI.

PROPOSITIONS FOR THE RE-MONETIZATION OF SILVER CONSIDERED.

A FEELING in favor of the use of silver, as an unlimited legal-tender money, appears to exist in parts of the country, and the restoration of the silver dollar of $412\frac{1}{2}$ grains is especially urged by some, for the reason that any contract or obligation involving the payment of "Dollars," "Coin," or "Lawful money," made prior to April 1, 1873, is legally dischargeable in silver dollars of that standard, as heretofore coined.

The advocates of the restoration of the old silver dollar do not appear to have in view the concurrent circulation of gold coins and the silver dollar under the double standard, on the ratio of 1 to 15.98+, which would be established by an Act authorizing its unrestricted coinage, and declaring it an unlimited tender. They appear to think that an error, if not a wrong, was committed in discontinuing its coinage;

and they desire to correct the same without reference to the question, whether it would be possible to maintain the concurrent circulation of gold and silver coins after resumption in 1879.

Others favor the adoption of a double standard on the ratio of 1 to $15\frac{1}{2}$, which would give a silver dollar of the standard weight of 400 grains, nearly. The chief and weighty reason given for adopting this ratio, or relative valuation, in the coinage is that it would place the United States in harmony with France, and other countries employing the double standard, and would offer a strong inducement for them to open their mints for the coinage of silver, and thereby restore its former value and bring the market relation of the two metals into substantial correspondence with their relative value in the coinage. This would require the gold price of silver to advance to, and remain at, about $60\frac{3}{4}$ pence per ounce British standard (.925 fine). The average price for several months past has been about 54 pence.

If Congress should authorize a dollar of either of these weights, and it should be coined on a large scale, the effect would be the gradual appreciation of silver as compared with gold, and this would continue as silver passed into use as money in this country, provided that France, and some other countries, should not seize the opportunity to abandon the double standard, and adopt that of gold alone. In that case, the support given to silver, by its coinage as a standard money in the United States, would be more than counterbalanced, and further depreciation would be likely to follow.

If a law should be passed authorizing the coinage of a legal-tender silver dollar for depositors, the coining rate of silver into dollar pieces would immediately become what is termed the "mint price of silver," and, until the market value of silver bullion should advance to that rate, gold coins would be at a premium. If such an advance should not take place, silver would become the actual standard, and gold would be excluded from the channels of circulation, and would in fact soon be known only to money brokers and exchange dealers.

It may well be doubted whether France and her monetary allies are likely, unless the silver standard should be adopted by the United States, to fully abrogate the double standard, although it is quite certain that they will not coin any silver until the greater portion of the German stock shall have first been distributed and absorbed.

The mints of Europe being closed against the coinage of legal-tender silver money, a market for that metal must be found principally in China and the Indies. If the demand for these countries is at any time large, the price of silver advances more or less, and recedes on the demand being met.

The lowest rate at which Germany will sell silver is understood to be 55 pence per ounce, 925 thousandths fine. The coining rate of a dollar of 400 grains, .900 fine, would correspond to $60\frac{13}{16}$ pence per ounce, .925 fine, and a dollar of $412\frac{1}{2}$ grains to 59 pence. The authorizing of the coinage of a legal-tender silver dollar for depositors would be the fixing of a mint price for silver payable in such dollars, and an invitation to the different countries to send us their silver, which, if fully responded to, would place us at once upon a silver standard.

At the outset it would be a depreciated standard, subject to appreciation, or further depreciation, according to the action which other countries might take in respect to their money standards.

Divested of technical terms and treated according to common sense, the money standard question may be briefly stated as follows:

1. Money, which is to serve as the measure of contracts and medium for effecting the exchange of all kinds of property, must consist of some tangible and comparatively imperishable substance, acceptable to, and recognized as money by, the various nations of the world. Gold and Silver have been found, by the experience of ages, to answer these requirements better than anything else.

2. Owing to the vast amount of gold and silver which has accumulated in the world, an increased or diminished product of either or both of these metals from the mines, for even a considerable period of time, does not ordinarily affect, to any perceptible degree, their value relatively to other things.

3. The exchange or purchasing power of the precious metals is due in a great degree to their long and almost universal employment as money.

4. Their relative value is more widely and quickly affected by the increased or diminished use of either as money than from all other causes. This has been strikingly exemplified in our own times by the change from the silver to the gold standard by the German Empire.

5. These metals are subject to changes in their relative value which render it difficult, if not impossible, to retain for a considerable period of time in any country the concurrent use of legal-tender coins of both metals in a fixed ratio.

6. If a double standard be adopted by a country, one or the other of the metals will, as a general rule, be used as the principal money of payment to the exclusion of the other. The cheapest money will generally be selected for payment, or, in other words, that metal which for the time being is the cheaper will be taken to the mint for coinage, while the other

will be exported. These conditions as to both metals may change in greater or less periods of time. The double standard may therefore be properly termed an alternate standard.

7. The greater the number, population and wealth of the countries adopting a double standard, on the same ratio or relative valuation, in their coinage, the greater would be the probability of maintaining it. Until such a system shall have been adopted by a number of the most important of the countries of the world, the United States should treat the question as one to be settled according to its own situation and requirements.

8. After resumption of specie payment, redeemable paper money will constitute the greater portion of the circulating medium, even if the present gold standard be adhered to; and if the silver standard should prevail, such paper money will no doubt be used to a much greater extent than would be the case under a gold standard, for the reason that a given value in silver would be about sixteen times as heavy as in gold, and proportionately inconvenient to handle, and on that account far less desirable than paper money.

The advantages of a single gold standard, with silver as a subordinate tender, compared with the double or alternate standard of gold and silver, would appear to be sufficient to justify this country in adhering to

5*

its present position with reference to the metallic money standard.

A change from the gold to the silver standard by the United States does not appear to be advocated by any one; but the issuing of a silver dollar on the old basis, or on that of a relative valuation of 1 to $15\frac{1}{2}$, as an unlimited tender and with unrestricted coinage, would probably place this country upon a silver standard for years to come.

The law may fix a legal-tender valuation of the two metals, on the assumption that one ounce of pure gold is of equal value with $15\frac{1}{2}$ or $15\frac{98}{100}$ ounces of pure silver, but if an ounce of pure gold will exchange for $17\frac{1}{2}$ ounces of pure silver in London, Paris, Amsterdam or Berlin, as at present, gold will leave America and silver will come to it, despite the law.

It may be claimed that our power to use silver for coinage would be sufficient to exhaust the German stock, and that gold leaving us and accumulating in the countries of the single gold standard, would cause it to depreciate, and that sooner or later the relative value of the two metals, which existed prior to the change of standard in Germany, would be restored. This might be the case, provided France, and other countries of the double standard, should adhere to the same, and re-open their mints for the unrestricted coinage of silver. As to what will be the course of these countries in respect to their money standard, no one can predict. The conjecture is that they will keep their mints closed against the coinage of silver, until the greater portion of the German stock, estimated at about $80,000,000, shall have been absorbed by other countries.

It is probable that about two years and a half more will be sufficient for the sale and absorption of the greater portion of this amount, at the end of which time the Monetary Convention or Union between France, Belgium, Italy and Switzerland will expire by its own limitation; and each of those nations will be left free to act for itself. At present they cannot, under the terms of the Convention, separately change the double standard which existed at the time it was signed.

In the mean time the position of France, the principal country of the Latin Monetary Union, is very peculiar, and deserves especial attention in connection with the money standard question. In estimating the amount of gold and silver in France, all authorities appear to agree that it exceeds, in proportion to her population, the specie held by any other country. It is also agreed that the specie in that country which could be readily called into effective use as money is double the amount of paper money outstanding.

The principal reason for deferring a return to specie

payments in France has been, no doubt, that it would result in a loss of gold, and a further accumulation of silver. That such would have been the result cannot be reasonably doubted; and this would continue as long as an ounce of gold could be exchanged in other countries for a greater number of ounces of silver than in France. This the French would not willingly endure, and that country may be expected to continue a policy required by her peculiar position.

The most available as well as effective measure, short of the change by law from the gold and silver standard to that of gold, would be the closing the French mints against the coinage of silver.

By this and other measures, France may continue to hold a stock of gold under a nominal double standard, notwithstanding the over-valuation of silver by her existing regulations.

That country has in the past made an earnest struggle for the maintenance of the gold and silver standard, and will probably adhere to that standard as long as it does not result in the export of gold. Whenever it comes to that, France may be expected to declare for the gold standard as promptly as she closed her mints to silver to prevent the same result.

The Netherlands and Belgium followed France in discontinuing the coinage of silver, and for the same purpose; and if France should adopt the single gold standard, those countries would undoubtedly find it necessary to take the same course.

France suspended the coinage of standard silver money within a comparatively short time after the conclusion of a disastrous war, and in the face of vast losses and debts. And in doing so, she refused abundant supplies of cheap money.

The United States, ten years after the close of a wasteful but successful war, discontinued the coinage of standard silver money, under conditions somewhat similar, and is now urged to retrace her steps.

Those who favor the re-monetization of silver in the United States differ only as to the quantity of pure metal to be contained in the silver dollar, and the ratio of value of gold to silver, which would be established by the passage of a law authorizing the unrestricted coinage of an unlimited legal-tender silver dollar. If a dollar of $412\frac{1}{2}$ grains standard silver be authorized, the coining rate or mint price of silver would be $116\frac{4}{11}$ cents per ounce, .900 fine, equivalent to 59 pence per ounce, .925 fine. The coining rate of a dollar of $399\frac{9}{10}$ grains would be 120 cents per standard ounce, equivalent to $60\frac{3}{4}$ pence British standard. Before a dollar of $412\frac{1}{2}$ grains would be of equal value with a gold dollar of $25\frac{8}{10}$ grains, the price of silver must advance to 59 pence, and to render a dol- of $399\frac{9}{10}$ grains of standard silver equal to the gold dollar, the price of silver must advance to 60¾ pence gold.

Accordingly if the issue of a dollar of either weight, with unrestricted coinage and tender be authorized, depositors of silver bullion would gain the difference between the actual gold value of the silver contained in the dollar and the nominal or legal-tender value of the latter. This would continue to be the case until prices generally should adapt themselves to the new standard, or the gold price of silver advance to a point which would make the silver and gold dollar of equal value. The gain would probably range for some time to come from a half of one per cent. to twelve per cent.

To allow private parties to realize any gain whatever from the coinage of money would be clearly wrong, and especially in the case of coins having a nominal or legal-tender value greater than their bullion value.

Whatever gain arises from the issue of such moneys should be realized by the Public Treasury, as representing the entire people, and until the price of silver should advance to a point which would make a silver dollar equal in value with a gold dollar, it is clear that the silver dollar, if authorized, should be coined and issued on account of the Treasury of the United States, and not for private parties.

As to the basis, or relative valuation, on which the proposed dollar should be coined, it may be said that if it were certain that France and other countries of the double standard would permanently adhere to the same, we should conform to the ratio already adopted by them, *i. e.*, 1 to $15\frac{1}{2}$, because it would give the system greater stability. But, as that is a matter of uncertainty, we ought for the present to assume and hold a conservative position, which would leave us free to adopt the ratio of 1 to $15\frac{1}{2}$ whenever the action of other countries should be such as to allow it to be done with safety.

By adopting the ratio of 1 to 15.98, the coining rate of silver would be about three per cent. less than under the ratio of 1 to $15\frac{1}{2}$; a difference sufficient to prevent the coins representing silver in the ratio of 1 to $15\frac{1}{2}$ from coming to our Mints; but this protection would not hold good if, at any time, the legal-tender character of such foreign coins should be removed or materially reduced by law.

Assuming that the legal tender of the existing standard silver coins of France and other countries of the double standard will not be disturbed, we would have the German stock and part of the annual production of the mines of Mexico and South America to deal with.

If we are to receive accumulated stocks of silver

from any source, and place a stamp, or legal-tender value, upon it higher than the market rate, it is important that we procure it at that rate, which can be done only by the purchase of the bullion by the Government, to be coined and issued on its own account.

If coined for individuals, the coining rate will be the rate at which it will come to us and be paid for by the Mints. We will suppose that Congress, after a full discussion of the subject, authorizes the coinage of a dollar of $412\frac{1}{2}$ grains, and declares it a legal tender, equally with United States notes, and directs the Secretary of the Treasury to have coined and issued, say, fifty million dollars, and that the bullion can be purchased and the coinage executed at a gain of about six per cent. We will suppose, further, that this amount of silver dollars be coined within two years, and enter fully into circulation, and that, at the end of that time, silver recovers its former relative value to gold, and that France and other countries of the double standard re-open their mints to the coinage of silver. Whenever the latter should take place, the silver dollar would of course be exported, and we would then be compelled to rely upon gold and redeemable paper money, or reduce the weight of the silver dollar to, say, 400 grains. Although such a reduction would bring all the existing dollars to the Mint for re-coinage, no disadvantage would result from the same, as the purchasing power of the dollar of reduced weight would be greater than the old dollar at the present time, and the excess of weight in the old coins would be amply sufficient to defray the expenses of re-coinage.

If, on the contrary, silver should not recover its former value, the amount issued would not be sufficient to produce any serious injury to public or private interests.

There is another and quite important point to be considered in connection with the proposed issue of a standard silver coin, and that is the distribution of the same to the different sections of the country.

If issued on account of the Government, the cost of transportation to all parts of the Union could be paid out of the gain arising from the re-coinage, and an equal and very general distribution would be insured; if coined for depositors, the coins would unduly accumulate in the cities and large towns, and find their way very slowly to the country districts.

This country would, no doubt, absorb a large amount of dollar coins, having the same legal tender power as United States notes, provided that individuals are not compelled to pay the cost of transporting them from the Mints.

As has already been stated, the law of March 18, 1869, "to strengthen the public credit," declared in positive terms all the then existing money obligations of the United States to be payable "in coin or its equivalent." The word "coin," as used in this Act, must be understood to refer to the coins of the United States, of the then existing conditions as to fineness, weight, value and legal tender, and embracing the gold coins of $25\frac{8}{10}$ grains, $\frac{9}{10}$ fine, to the dollar, and the silver dollar of $421\frac{1}{2}$ grains, and same fineness.

On the 14th of July, 1870, an Act "to authorize the refunding of the national debt" was approved, which authorized the sale, exchange and issue of prescribed amounts of 5, $4\frac{1}{2}$ and 4 per cent. bonds, redeemable in "coin of the present standard value," at the pleasure of the United States, after certain periods named, the interest payable in such coin. Strictly construed, the words "coin of the present standard value," as used in this Act, must be regarded as meaning the full legal-tender coins which at the time represented the money of account, *i. e.*, all the gold coins coined at the rate of $25\frac{8}{10}$ grains, $\frac{9}{10}$ fine, to the dollar, and the silver dollar of $412\frac{1}{2}$ grains of the same fineness.

Payment of the principal and interest of bonds, issued under this Act, must be in gold coins containing $23\frac{22}{100}$ grains of fine gold to the dollar, or silver dollars containing $371\frac{1}{4}$ grains fine silver.

The coinage of silver dollars having been discontinued by the Coinage Act of 1873, and a very limited portion of those coined prior to that year having escaped the melting-pot, payment of the bonds can be made only in gold coins, unless the coinage of such dollars, with unlimited tender, should again be authorized.

The object in using the peculiar phraseology,—"coins of the present standard value,"—appears to have been to insure the purchaser of the bonds against the possibility of being compelled to receive either principal or interest in coins containing less fine bullion than those in which their subscriptions were to be paid. In other words, payment, according to the metallic money standard of that date, was in terms expressly provided for.

It is a well known fact that settlement for all bonds, issued under the provisions of this Act, has without exception been made on the basis of $25\frac{8}{10}$ grains of standard, or $23\frac{22}{100}$ grains of fine gold to the coined dollar, and the purchasers and holders of such bonds very naturally expect to receive payment in "gold coins of standard value" equal to the coins in which their subscriptions were made and paid.

In connection with this question, it should be stated that, for nearly thirty-six years previous to the passage of the Refunding Act, gold had been generally recognized, particularly in Europe, as the actual money standard of this country, and the silver dollar coin was considered practically obsolete.

Notwithstanding the option as to payment in gold coin or silver dollars given the Government by the law, the fact that the bonds have been taken and settled for on the gold basis, and that silver, in the mean time, comparing its commercial value with that fixed by law in the silver dollar, has materially depreciated, renders it very doubtful, to say the least, whether the United States could with justice pay either the principal or interest of its bonds in silver dollars.

If the Treasury had sold the bonds, and received payment on the basis of silver dollars, of the weight and fineness existing by law in 1870, it might justly redeem in such dollars; but to do so, in face of the undisputed fact that it received payment on the gold basis, ($25\tfrac{8}{10}$ grains standard to the dollar,) would be to subject its good faith to suspicion, as well as to disregard its moral obligation to return borrowed money equivalent in all respects to that which it received. Moreover, since the passage of the Coinage Act of 1873, many bonds have been sold and have changed hands, and no silver coins have been in existence of a legal-tender character with which to pay them, and it would be a breach of good faith to compel such holders to receive a coin which was not then in existence, and which they had no reason to expect would ever be in existence.

Whenever the market value of the two metals shall be such that $371\frac{1}{4}$ grains of pure silver will exchange for or purchase $23\frac{22}{100}$ grains of pure gold, it will not matter which metal is used in payment, as either will then be an equivalent for that which the creditor paid and the United States received, but until that relative valuation shall again be reached, the people of this country cannot afford, even though the law give the right, to compel creditors to accept $371\frac{1}{4}$ grains of pure silver for the $23\frac{22}{100}$ grains pure gold, which was borrowed from them.

It may be stated as a fundamental principle that a metallic money standard once fairly established cannot, without violating the equity of existing money obligations, be appreciated or depreciated by law.

It sometimes happens that a nation, by the issue of irredeemable legal-tender notes, departs for a time from its metallic standard. Such a departure operates to the disadvantage of creditors the moment the issue is sufficient in amount to produce depreciation. The depreciation of such a currency, or legal-tender paper money, is shown by a general rise in prices.

Whenever such legal-tender credit-money has once been issued in excess, it becomes the actual money standard on which the business of the country is conducted; all obligations involving the payment of money being, as a general rule, based upon it. When this artificial standard has prevailed for a considerable time, a return to the latent or dormant metallic standard becomes a matter of great difficulty, and must be attended, even under the most favorable circumstances, with much suffering on the part of debtors, as well as a general depression of business.

If a nation may not depart from its metallic money standard, except as a last resort for its own preservation, it surely should not undertake to return too rapidly to the metallic standard; especially where there has been a wide departure from it. Years of industry and frugality on the part of the people, as well as a wise and economical administration of public affairs, are necessary to bring a country from a depreciated paper money to the metallic standard previously existing, however great may be its natural resources. This is shown in the United States, where a credit-money standard, which has prevailed since 1862, has not yet been brought to a parity with the metallic standard.

Some advantage would result from the coinage of a silver dollar, but nothing like what is claimed for it. Being too heavy to be handled and carried about, it would find a place in bank and treasury vaults, rather than in the hands of the people.

If coined without restriction or limitation of legal tender, silver will, as far as can now be seen, become the actual money standard to the exclusion of gold. This it is clear we cannot afford.

If the coinage of the silver dollar is to be authorized, the true policy would appear to be to place such restrictions upon its issue and its legal-tender character as will prevent the depreciation of United States notes before resumption, or the expulsion of gold from the country after resumption.

Notwithstanding twelve years only have elapsed since the close of the war which called the issue of legal-tender credit-money into existence, the public credit has been gradually improved, until a near approach to the metallic standard has been effected,—a result alike honorable to the people and Government of the United States. In view of this creditable achievement, and of the unquestionable advantages of a metallic standard over one of irredeemable paper money, it cannot be doubted that our true policy is to keep the resumption of specie payments steadily in view, and avoid all doubtful measures, even though they should promise temporary advantages.

Whenever the value of United States notes shall have fairly risen to par, whether through compulsory redemption, or as a result of a specific date having been fixed by law for such redemption, or from other causes, the gold coin of the country, now in a dormant condition, will be brought into active use as money, and will not only produce a healthy stimulation of all industries, but lay a secure foundation for a general and permanent prosperity.

A careful survey of the money situation of Europe clearly indicates an early relaxation in the demand for gold for coinage purposes. Great Britain, Germany, France, the Netherlands, Belgium, and the Scandinavian States, are all well supplied with gold money. Russia, Austria, Italy and Spain, have a paper-money standard and will be compelled to retain it for an indefinite period, and the European demand for silver must necessarily be quite limited for some years to come. In fact the tendency, except in the countries first named, is everywhere in Europe in the direction of increased issues of irredeemable paper money and the cheapening of both gold and silver.

In our own country there is at least $175,000,000 of gold coin and bullion, and the annual gold product of our mines is, say, $45,000,000. Of silver coin, there is about $40,000,000 in circulation, and the annual product from the mines approximates $35,000,000. Moreover, the balance of trade is now in our favor and likely to continue so. Altogether the situation is much more favorable than for some years past, for the acquisition of the amount of precious metals required for placing the finances of the country on a metallic basis. Of gold, which should be our money of large payments, we have already the greater portion necessary; and silver, which with us will find its true place in small payments and trade coin, will be produced from our own mines, and come to us from other countries, more rapidly than we can coin it.

Let the statesmen of America see to it that the opportunity be not lost.

APPENDIX.

(A).—AGGREGATE PRODUCTION OF SILVER.

(B).—GENERAL SUMMARY OF THE MOVEMENTS OF SILVER.

(C).—USE OF SILVER FOR PURPOSES OF MANUFACTURE.

(D).—NATIONS AND POPULATIONS UNDER THE THREE SYSTEMS (GOLD; GOLD AND SILVER; SILVER).

(E).—THE RIGHT TO COIN MONEY.

(F).—COINS OF THE UNITED STATES; AUTHORITY FOR COINING AND CHANGES IN WEIGHT AND FINENESS.

(G).—THE RATIOS OF GOLD TO SILVER FROM 1760 TO 1833.

(H).—YEARLY AVERAGES OF THE PRICE OF SILVER FROM 1834 TO 1876, ETC.

(I).—TOTAL COINAGE OF THE UNITED STATES MINTS TO JUNE 30, 1877.

(A)

AGGREGATE PRODUCTION OF SILVER.

[From the Report of a Select Committee of the House of Commons on Depreciation of Silver.]

Interesting statistics have been submitted to your Committee with regard to the aggregate production, both of gold and silver. Calculations have also been put in evidence with reference to the relative proportions in which gold and silver have been respectively produced at various periods, and the attention of your Committee was called to the fact that, speaking very broadly, silver was produced, as compared with gold, in the proportion of 3 to 1 during the earlier part of the century; that the proportion fell to .68 to 1 in 1848; to .27 to 1 between 1852 and 1856; and that between 1857 and 1875 it gradually rose to .68 to 1. It will be observed that according to these computations, notwithstanding the late rise in the production of silver, as compared with gold, its proportion to gold is still considerably below what it was in 1848, to say nothing of the period when the proportion was 3 to 1; and the conclusion seems justified, that a review of the "relations of the metals in times past shows that the fall in the price of silver is not due to any excessive production as *compared with gold.*" The fact is that, as was correctly pointed out by Mr. Giffen in his evidence, the changes have been *in the uses of the metals.* Gold has come more generally into use than before, and indeed the condition of trade and the situation of various countries using gold and silver respectively have entirely changed. Arguments based on the relative yield of gold and silver mines have accordingly become very misleading, and your Committee did not think it expedient to pursue this branch of inquiry (complicated as it is by almost insurmountable difficulties of computation) beyond the point to which they have here called attention. They have confined themselves to the consideration of such estimates as bear on the production of silver.

All computations of the aggregate production of any metal over a series of years must be treated with great caution, and as mere estimates. Accurate information as to all sources of supply cannot be obtained, and the inferences to be drawn from such statistics can only be of a general character. With this reservation, your Committee draw attention to the following figures supplied by Sir Hector Hay, an eminent bullion-broker, as to the aggregate production of silver in the world since the year 1852.

In the period 1852 to 1862, the annual production of silver is estimated to have ranged between £8,000,000 and £9,000,000.

In 1862 it is believed to have reached £9,040,000
" 1863 " " " " 9,840,000
" 1864 " " " " 10,340,000
" 1867 " " " " 10,845,000

Between 1868 and 1870 the amounts were somewhat lower; and since then the figures given are:

For 1871 £12,210,000
" 1872 13,050,000
" 1873 14,050,000
" 1874 14,300,000
" 1875 16,100,000

For the years up to 1873 Sir Hector Hay appears to have included in his totals the amounts given for the United States by Mr. Raymond, the "Commissioner for Mining Statistics;" but for the years 1874 and 1875 he had not the final official estimates of that authority before him. Those estimates have now been received, and, when substituted for the figures previously given, bring down the totals:

For the year 1874 to £13,500,000
" " 1875 " 14,200,000

Your Committee, in a subsequent part of their report, discuss the probable production of the mines of the United States during the last two years, and examine the discrepancies in the various estimates; but even on the basis of the lowest figures, the immense increase from an annual average of between £8,000,000 and £9,000,000 to the sum of £14,200,000, will be at once observed.

According to every estimate the increase in the production since 1870 is wholly accounted for by the increased yield in the mines of the United States.

The latest estimates of the Commissioner for Mining Statistics of the yield of these mines are the following:

1859	£20,000	1870	£3,200,000
1860	30,000	1871	4,600,000
1861	400,000	1872	5,750,000
1862	900,000	1873	7,150,000
1863	1,700,000	1874	6,400,000
1864–1869, average	2,325,000	1875	6,400,000

The production of silver in Mexico and South America is represented to have been very steady. The annual amount is estimated at £6,000,000 for the years between 1852 and 1867. It has since been supposed to have fallen to £5,000,000, notwithstanding a decided increase in the Caracoles Mines. Except for this circumstance, if the figures are at all trustworthy, the decline in the yield would have been greater.

The silver productions of all other countries has also been represented to your Committee as comparatively stationary since 1862. It is taken at a little over £2,000,000 annually.

The estimates for the total production are therefore as follows:

In the years previous to any supplies from the
    United States—Mexico and South America   £6,000,000
    Other Countries.   2,000,000

                                            Total   £8,000,000

In the years 1864 to 1867, when the yield in the
    United States had considerably developed,
    United States   £2,300,000
    Mexico and South America   6,000,000
    Other Countries   2,000,000

                                            Total   £10,300,000

In 1872,
    United States   £5,750,000
    Mexico and South America   5,200,000
    Other Countries   2,000,000

                                            Total   £12,950,000

In 1874,
    United States   £6,400,000
    Mexico and South America   5,000,000
    Other Countries   2,000,000

                                            Total   £13,400,000

To arrive at the present time at the total annual production of silver, the yield of all other countries should be taken at about £7,000,000 and the production of the United States should be added to that amount.

(B)

GENERAL SUMMARY OF THE MOVEMENTS OF SILVER.

[Continuation of Parliamentary Report.]

Your Committee have now passed under review the movements of silver in all countries where information was available, with the object of showing which countries have absorbed the large supplies which have been produced during the last four years, or added to the amount produced by the disposal of surplus stocks.

If the statements made with regard to the separate countries be put together, the general account will be as follows, the figures being mainly derived from official documents, but nevertheless, doubtless, open to much criticism:

	1872-1875.
Total production	£54,700,000
Sold by Germany and Scandinavian Kingdoms in consequence of changes in currency about	8,000,000
Surplus of Exports over Imports in Italy during 1872 and 1873	8,000,000
Ditto in Austria 1872-1875	4,000,000
	£74,700,000

	1872–1875.
Taken by India	£9,100,000
" " France	33,500,000
" " Russia	4,000,000
" " Spain and Portugal	4,000,000
" " England	5,000,000
" " United States	7,600,000
" " Japan and the East	7,500,000
" " The East (other than India, China and Japan)	3,000,000
	£73,700,000

Your Committee only submit this statement as a general sketch. The investigation is so complicated, and surrounded with so many difficulties, and the statistics so incomplete in many instances, that it is very remarkable that the figures so nearly balance, but they are rather valuable as showing the general tendencies of the market, and the ebb and flow in the movement of silver, than as actual historical data.

(C)

USE OF SILVER FOR PURPOSES OF MANUFACTURE.

[Continuation of Parliamentary Report.]

Your Committee, in the course of their inquiry, have had to consider to what extent, if any, the disuse of silver for articles of plate, and the well known substitution of electroplated manufactures in their place might have contributed to the fall in the price of silver. They did not pursue this subject into any detail, as it appeared that the total quantities in question used in Europe were comparatively too small to exercise much influence on the market in comparison with the immense operations connected with the use of silver as a circulating medium. Evidence obtained from the Inland Revenue Office showed the amount of manufactured silver on which duty has been charged over a series of years. Certain articles are excepted, but the details as to the amount of duty levied are a complete indication of the quantity used for plate. An extract from the 13th Report of the Commissioners of Inland Revenue, shows on what articles the duty is charged, what are exempted articles, how the duty is raised, and what is the mode of its collection. It will be seen that it is collected at the Assay-offices, which are in the following cities and towns: London, Birmingham, Sheffield, Exeter, Newcastle, Chester, York, Edinburgh, Glasgow, and Dublin. In London the work is done by the Goldsmiths' Company. Returns have been received from all the Assay-Offices, and also statements from the Inland Revenue, and from the Statistical Department of the Custom-House. Mr. Seyd also put in a paper based on official information.

The amount of foreign plate imported is so small as scarcely to merit mention. How far the duty of 1s. 6d. per ounce on silver plate, whether manufactured abroad or at home, interferes with the manufacture, is an open question which your Committee did not pursue. The annual quantity of foreign silver plate imported ranged between 50,000 and 90,000 ounces, except the year 1871, when, in consequence of the war in France, the amount was somewhat increased, and reached 103,000 ounces.

The quantity of silver plate manufactured at home and exported is also very small. The amount of plate on which drawback was allowed in the year 1852 was about 150,000 ounces; in the year 1875 it was 120,000 ounces. The value of the silver used, taken at 60*d.*, would only be £30,000, allowing for the fact that the duty is only paid on five-sixths of the weight.

The amount retained for home use was in 1852 725,000 ounces; in 1874, 730,000; in 1875, 766,000 ounces. No change of any amount is apparent in these figures. The use of electroplate appears to have had but the slightest effect on the total quantities of silver plate manufactured as far as these statistics show.

And with regard to the total, it will be seen that, taking the gross weight of silver marked at Goldsmiths' Hall and the other Assay-offices, it does not exceed about 1,300,000 ounces, or, at 60*d.*, £325,000. Taking into account the amount imported, the total does not reach £350,000 actually retained for use in England. To this, however, it is necessary to add what is used for electroplating and other manufacture. Mr. Seyd estimates this quantity as under 1,000,000 ounces. This amount, calculating on the old value of the metal, viz.: 60*d.* per ounce, on which all the estimates of production and supply have been framed, is £250,000. The result would accordingly be a total of £600,000.

The consumption in France is probably rather larger, as more "solid articles" are used.

The great consumption of silver plate in the United Kingdom is among the higher classes; but in France, as well as in Germany, it is among the lower classes. The German peasantry, for instance, are in the habit of collecting a certain amount of silver spoons, which they treat as dowries for their daughters.

It is unfortunately impossible to obtain any trustworthy information on this subject. Mr. Seyd spoke of very exaggerated statements, which had been made elsewhere, with regard to an enormous consumption of silver for manufacturing purposes. Your Committee were inclined to think that he, on the other hand, somewhat underestimated the amount. If an amount of about £600,000 be the correct amount for England, the sum of £2,000,000 per annum for the whole of Europe would appear rather small. In any case there is no appearance of such fluctuations in the quantity as would count for much in the movements of the European markets.

FINAL SUMMARY.

To sum up the more striking facts which have been brought before your Committee, the situation at the present moment appears to be this:

1. The total annual production of silver has risen to upwards of £14,000,000, from an average of about £8,000,000 to £9,000,000 in 1860.

2. Of this amount of £14,000,000, the mines of the United States are estimated to have produced about £7,000,000, with the prospect of an increase for some years to come. On the other hand, if the price of silver should remain as low as at present, there may be some diminution in the production elsewhere.

3. Germany has still to dispose of an amount which is certainly not less than £8,000,000, with the possibility that it may exceed £20,000,000; but with the possibility, on the other hand, that a considerably larger sum than the estimated amount may be ultimately required for subsidiary coinage.

4. The Scandinavian Kingdoms have discontinued the use of silver; but the amounts of demonetized silver coin which they have thrown, or can throw, on the market are not important.

5. Austria has apparently been exchanging silver for gold, the amount of silver held in the Imperial Bank having diminished from £10,000,000 to £6,600,000 since 1871.

6. Italy has been gradually denuded of her silver currency. Since 1865 large amounts have been exported; her forced paper currency has apparently expelled the whole of the metallic currency, of which the silver coins amounted, at the beginning of 1866, to about £17,000,000.

7. France, on the other hand, has for some years past been replenishing her stock of silver, of which during the last four years her imports have exceeded her exports by £33,500,000.

8. England, Russia and Spain have each been buyers to the extent of some millions.

9. Japan and China, and other countries in the East, have absorbed a certain amount.

10. India still takes silver, but in greatly decreased amounts.

11. The Home Government has bills to sell to the amount of £15,000,000 per annum, which debtors to India can buy in the place of remitting bullion. This total has been gradually reached, and represents an excess of more than £10,000,000, compared with twenty years ago.

12. The gross remittances of silver to India during the last four years have been £15,600,000, compared with £28,900,000 in the four previous years.

Legislatively, the position is as follows:

Germany is gradually demonetizing silver, and looks forward to its use only for subsidiary coinage.

The United States is carrying out a policy of introducing silver subsidiary coinage in the place of all fractional paper currency now afloat, . . . and only available for legal tender for a limited amount.

The members of the Latin Union and Holland have adopted an expectant attitude; but meanwhile limit, as far as possible, the coinage of silver.

No indications are given of any intention on the part of Russia and Austria to pass any laws with regard to their currency.

The actual facts which have been enumerated speak for themselves; and it will be seen at once which of them are in favor of a rise in the price of silver, and which of them tend in a contrary direction. It is important, too, that the temporary character of some of these facts, and the normal character of others, should be fully taken into account. The surplus stock of Germany will, in all probability, weigh heavily on the market for some time to come, still it is a temporary circumstance. On the other hand, the United States will afford temporary relief to the market by retaining, for her own coinage, considerable amounts of the silver there produced. It is indeed possible, according to the evidence adduced, that the United States will retain as much silver for her new coinage operations as Germany may have to sell as the result of hers.

The case of France deserves especial attention. The replenishment of her stock of silver can scarcely be regarded as other than a temporary circumstance. During the last four years, out of a total of £76,000-

000 of disposable silver, France absorbed £33,500,-000. The relief thereby given to the market must have been immense. It is impossible to assume that it can be continued on the same scale. The natural inference to be drawn would be in the opposite direction.

With regard to India and the East, hitherto the largest consumers of silver, so much must depend upon the prosperity of the populations, on the abundance of the crops, in fact, on their powers of production, that it is impossible to make any forecast; and as regards actual facts, no more can be stated than that, on the other hand, they have always possessed a very large power of absorbing bullion, while on the other, that power has been diminished by the growth of the sums annually payable by India to the Home Government.

The only facts in any calculation as to the future which are certain, and appear to be permanent, are the increased total production of silver, and the effect caused by the necessity of the Indian Government to draw annually for a heavy amount. Both are adverse to the future value of silver, as far as they go; but they may be partially counterbalanced by changes in the trade with the East.

As regards Europe, much must depend upon the action taken by the governments of the various countries where the question of the currency to be adopted is still unsettled. Your Committee have not considered it to be within the scope of the questions referred to them to make inquiry as to the intentions of these governments, though many references to their views will be found in the various official documents procured for the Committee by the Foreign Office. Your Committee on this point would simply remark, that it is obvious that if effect should be given to the policy of substituting gold for silver, whenever it is feasible, and giving gold, for the sake of its advantages in international commerce, the preference even among populations whose habits and customs are in favor of silver, and thus displacing silver from the position (which it has always occupied) of doing the work of the currency over at least as large an area as gold, no possible limits could be assigned to the further fall in its value, which would inevitably take place; but your Committee are bound to refrain from giving any opinion on the expediency of such a policy, or the necessity for its adoption.

In conclusion, your Committee have to observe that while they have endeavored to be as precise as possible in their statement of the facts which have been brought to their notice, and to give an explicit answer to the questions referred to them as to the causes of the present depreciation of silver, they consider that in view of the many uncertain elements to which they have pointed, and which necessarily enter into every calculation as to the future, they are not authorized to offer any further opinion as to the probable course of the silver market, beyond indicating, as they have endeavored to do, the various circumstances which have to be taken into account.

(D)

TABLE I. TABLES SUBMITTED BY MR. ERNEST SEYD, SHOWING THE NATIONS AND POPULATIONS (EXCLUSIVE OF SO-CALLED SAVAGES) UNDER THE THREE SYSTEMS IN 1871.

[Continuation of Parliamentary Report.]

Under the GOLD System.

	Population.
England	32,000,000
Portugal	4,000,000
Turkey	27,000,000
Persia	4,400,000
Australia	1,950,000
Cape and Canada	4,370,000
Brazil	10,200,000
Argentine	1,800,000
Total	85,720,000

Under GOLD and SILVER System.

	Population.
France	36,200,000
Belgium	5,100,000
Switzerland	2,700,000
Amount carried forward	44,000,000

	Population.
Amount brought forward	44,000,000
Italy	26,800,000
Spain	16,400,000
Greece	1,400,000
Roumania	4,000,000
United States	38,600,000
Columbia	2,900,000
Venezuela	1,600,000
Chili	1,900,000
Uruguay	400,000
Paraguay	1,200,000
Total	139,200,000

Under SILVER *System.*

	Population.
Germany	41,100,000
Holland	3,700,000
Denmark	1,800,000
Sweden	4,300,000
Norway	1,700,000
Austria	36,000,000
Russia	76,000,000
Egypt	4,500,000
Mexico	9,200,000
West Indies	600,000
Central America	2,600,000
Bolivia	1,800,000
Ecuador	1,300,000
Peru	3,400,000
Japan	33,000,000
China	425,000,000
India, etc.	195,000,000
Total	841,000,000

APPENDIX.

This table represents the *status quo* upon which, up to 1872, the supplies of both gold and silver were absorbed, the equilibrium, in accord with prices and requirements per head of population, being upheld by the three groups of equal aggregate weight each.

The totals of gold and silver in use as money, viz: coin in circulation, coin and bars held by banks and in the markets (exclusive of jewelry, plate and quantities supposed to be hoarded) may be given as follows:

Population.	In 1871. Under	Quantities in millions sterling.		
		Gold, full value.	Silver, full value.	Silver, as change.
85,720,000	Gold system,	160	40	26.5
139,200,000	Gold and silver system,	340	121	31.5
841,000,000	Silver system,	133	354	87
	Not accounted for since,	68	—	—
		49	16	—
		750	505	145

Among the gold-valuing states England and Australia only have a fully effective national system. The stock in England may be given as amounting to £130,000,000 of gold, and £15,000,000 of silver tokens. Of the other gold-valuing states, Portugal is dependent on England; the rest are under paper valuation or disorganization; and all excepting England and Australia, yet use between them about £14,000,000 of foreign silver coins of full value.

Among the gold and silver-valuing countries, France and Belgium take the lead, holding £275,000,000 of gold and £80,000,000 of full-valued silver. Of the silver systems, Germany and Holland in Europe, and India in the East occupy the guiding positions. Of the other states of both the latter systems, some are of second rank, others, like the United States, Russia, Italy, Austria, etc., have a paper valuation and possess but little metal, or practical influence at the moment on that score.

The following figures show the population and quantities for Europe alone in 1871:

Population.	In Europe in 1871. Under	Quantities in millions sterling.		
		Gold, full value.	Silver, full value.	Silver, as change.
48,000,000	Gold system,	138	4	22
92,600,000	Gold and silver system,	305	116	23.5
164,500,000	Silver system,	77	85	34.5
		520	205	80

The following figures show the population and quantities for the British Empire in 1871:

Population.	In British Empire in 1871. Under	Quantities in millions sterling.		
		Gold, full value.	Silver, full value.	Silver, as change.
38,000,000	Gold system,	146	—	16.9
196,000,000	Silver system,	15	170	25
		161	170	41.9

In reality the equilibrium maintained up to 1872 depended on the four states, England, France, Germany and India. All other states are of secondary importance, and in my opinion compelled to follow the lead taken by the four.

So long as between England with gold valuation, France with gold and silver valuation, Germany with silver valuation, both metals were upheld for the purposes of legal-tender money, the international value of silver remained secure for India.

The table now following shows the altered position and proportions of populations since 1871. For its appreciation the remarks following thereon are of importance.

TABLE II., SHOWING THE CHANGES IN THE THREE SYSTEMS DECIDED BY LAW, AND IN ABEYANCE SINCE 1871.

Under GOLD *System.*

	Population.
England	32,000,000
Portugal	4,000,000
Turkey	27,000,000
Persia	4,400,000
Australia	1,950,000
Cape and Canada	4,370,000
Brazil	10,200,000
Argentine.	1,800,000

Joined:

	Population.
Germany	41,100,000
Denmark	1,800,000
Sweden	4,300,000
Norway	1,700,000
United States	38,600,000

In abeyance:

Holland	3,700,000
France	36,200,000
Belgium	5,100,000
Switzerland	2,700,000
Italy	26,800,000
Total	247,720,000

Under GOLD and SILVER System.

	Population.
Spain	16,400,000
Greece	1,400,000
Roumania	4,000,000
Columbia	2,900,000
Venezuela	1,600,000
Chili	1,900,000
Uruguay	400,000
Paraguay	1,200,000

In abeyance:

Austria	36,000,000
Japan	33,000,000
Total	98,800,000

Under SILVER System.

	Population.
Russia	76,000,000
Egypt	4,500,000
Amount carried forward	80,500,000

		Population.
Amount brought forward		80,500,000
Mexico		9,200,000
West Indies		600,000
Central America		2,600,000
Ecuador		1,300,000
Peru		3,400,000
China		425,000,000
India		195,000,000
	Total	717,600,000

It is of paramount importance to bear in mind that Germany alone has actually succeeded in effecting a real change, *i. e.*, in acquiring gold and in disposing of a portion of its silver; and that it has had a payment of war indemnity of 200 millions sterling. But even in Germany the gold valuation is not yet complete; more gold is wanted, and silver remains to be sold.

The Scandinavian States have made but little progress in selling silver and obtaining gold.

The United States have no power to hold gold before they resume specie payments.

Holland and the Latin Union have been added to the gold-valuing list "in abeyance," the steps taken so far justifying this. Involved in the facts of the whole case, is the consideration: are these states compelled to follow the course of Germany? It will be found that (unless silver is re-monetized) they must do so for the sake of self-preservation. And as soon as a final decision is arrived at, the matter can no longer remain in suspense, but must become a reality, not only with the states which have so far legally decided, but have done little as yet, but with those in abeyance and those which have not yet moved.

The equilibrium dependent until 1872, as by Table I, on the proportions of, in Europe only:

	Gold system.	Gold and silver system.	Silver system.
Population, in millions and decimals,	48.0	92.6	164.5
Actually changed, as by Table II, by law in 1876, to	130.0	92.6	109.5
And with the five states in abeyance, equal to,	177.5	21.8	106.8

The change without reference to the states which have not yet moved, forms the basis or an estimate as to the re-distribution of gold, and the sales of silver required.

As regards the silver to be disposed of, it may be stated that, in 1871, Germany had a stock of £60,-000,000 to spare, the Latin Union, £92,000,000, and Holland, £9,000,000 in hand. Since then, according to the Government Statement, Germany has returned or parted with £31,000,000 of French, Belgian and Dutch pieces. This partly accounts for the rapid reduction of the German stocks, but increases those of France, Belgium and Holland. Together with the new coinages since made, the stock of full-valued silver liable to demonetization in the Latin Union and Holland is between £130,000,000 to £140,000,000. Besides this, Germany has yet silver to sell, as well as Scandinavia, and that of other European states remains behind.

(E)

THE RIGHT TO COIN MONEY.

[Extract from the Federalist. James Madison.]

. . . "The right of coining money, which is here taken from the States, was left in their hands by the Confederation, as a concurrent right with that of Congress, under an exception in favor of the exclusive right of Congress to regulate the alloy and value. In this instance, also, the new provision is an improvement on the old. Whilst the alloy and value depended on the general authority, a right of coinage in the particular States could have no other effect than to multiply expensive mints, and diversify the forms and weights of the circulating pieces. The latter inconveniency defeats one purpose for which the power was originally submitted to the Federal Head; and as far as the former might prevent an inconvenient remittance of gold and silver to the central mint for re-coinage, the end can be as well attained by local mints established under the general authority.

The extension of the prohibition to bills of credit, must give pleasure to every citizen, in proportion to his love of justice, and his knowledge of the true springs of public prosperity. The loss which America has sustained, since the peace, from the pestilent effects of paper money on the necessary confidence between man and man, on the necessary confidence in the public councils, on the industry and morals of the people, and on the character of republican government, constitutes an enormous debt against the States chargeable with this unadvised measure, which must long remain unsatisfied; or rather an accumulation of guilt, which can be expiated no otherwise than by a voluntary sacrifice on the altar of justice of the power which has been the instrument of it. In addition to these persuasive considerations, it may be observed that the same reasons which show the necessity of denying to the States the power of regulating coin prove, with equal force, that they ought not to be at liberty to substitute a paper medium in the place of coin. Had every State a right to regulate the value of its coin, there might be as many different currencies as States; and thus the intercourse among them would be impeded; retrospective alterations in its value might be made, and thus the citizens of other States be injured, and animosities be kindled among the States themselves. The subjects of foreign powers might suffer from the same cause, and hence the Union be discredited and embroiled by the indiscretion of a single member. No one of these mischiefs is less incident to a power in the States to emit paper money, than to coin gold or silver. The power to make anything but gold and silver a tender in payment of debts is withdrawn from the States, on the same principle with that of issuing a paper currency." . . .

(F)

COINS OF THE UNITED STATES, AUTHORITY FOR COINING, AND CHANGES IN WEIGHT AND FINENESS

Gold Coins.

DOUBLE-EAGLE.—Authorized to be coined, Act of March 3, 1849. Weight, 516 grains; fineness, 900.

EAGLE.—Authorized to be coined, Act of April 2, 1792. Weight, 270 grains; fineness, $916\frac{2}{3}$. Weight changed, Act of June 28, 1834, to 258 grains. Fineness changed, Act of June 28, 1834, to 899.225. Fineness changed, Act of January 18, 1837, to 900.

HALF-EAGLE.—Authorized to be coined, Act of April 2, 1792. Weight, 135 grains; fineness, $916\frac{2}{3}$. Weight changed, Act of June 28, 1834, to 129 grains. Fineness changed, Act of June 28, 1834, to 899.225. Fineness changed, Act of January 18, 1837, to 900.

QUARTER-EAGLE.—Authorized to be coined, Act of April 2, 1792. Weight, 67.5 grains; fineness, $916\frac{2}{3}$. Weight changed, Act of June 28, 1834, to

64.5 grains. Fineness changed, Act of June 28, 1834, to 899.225. Fineness changed, Act of January 18, 1837, to 900.

THREE-DOLLAR PIECE.—Authorized to be coined, Act of February 21, 1853. Weight, 77.4 grains; fineness, 900.

ONE DOLLAR.—Authorized to be coined, Act of March 3, 1849. Weight, 25.8 grains; fineness, 900.

Silver Coins.

DOLLAR.—Authorized to be coined, Act of April 2, 1792. Weight, 416 grains; fineness, 892.4. Weight changed, Act of January 18, 1837, to $412\frac{1}{2}$ grains. Fineness changed, Act of January 18, 1837, to 900. Coinage discontinued, Act of February 12, 1873.

TRADE DOLLAR.—Authorized to be coined, Act of February 12, 1873. Weight, 420 grains; fineness, 900.

HALF-DOLLAR.—Authorized to be coined, Act of April 2, 1792. Weight, 208 grains; fineness, 892.4. Weight changed, Act of Janurary 18, 1837, to $206\frac{1}{4}$ grains. Fineness changed, Act of January 18, 1837, to 900. Weight changed, Act of February 21, 1853, to 192 grains. Weight changed, Act of February 12, 1873, to $12\frac{1}{2}$ grams, or 192.9 grains.

QUARTER-DOLLAR.—Authorized to be coined,

Act of April 2, 1792. Weight, 104 grains; fineness, 892.4. Weight changed, Act of January 18, 1837, to $103\frac{1}{8}$ grains. Fineness changed, Act of January 18, 1837, to 900. Weight changed, Act of February 21, 1853, to 96 grains. Weight changed, Act of February 12, 1873, to $6\frac{1}{4}$ grams, or 96.45 grains.

TWENTY-CENT PIECE.—Authorized to be coined, Act of March 3, 1875. Weight, 5 grams, or 77.16 grains; fineness, 900.

DIME.—Authorized to be coined, Act of April 2, 1792. Weight, 41.6 grains; fineness, 892.4. Weight changed, Act of January 18, 1837, to $41\frac{1}{4}$ grains. Fineness changed, Act of January 18, 1837, to 900. Weight changed, Act of February 21, 1853, to 38.4 grains. Weight changed, Act of February 12, 1873, to $2\frac{1}{2}$ grams, or 38.58 grains.

HALF-DIME.—Authorized to be coined, Act of April 2, 1792. Weight, 20.8 grains; fineness, 892.4. Weight changed, Act of January 18, 1837, to $20\frac{5}{8}$ grains. Fineness changed, Act of January 18, 1837, to 900. Weight changed, Act of February 21, 1853, to 19.2 grains. Coinage discontinued, Act of February 12, 1873.

THREE-CENT PIECE.—Authorized to be coined, Act of March 3, 1851. Weight, $12\frac{3}{8}$ grains; fineness, 750. Weight changed, Act of March 3, 1853, to 11.52 grains. Fineness changed, Act of March 3,

1853, to 900. Coinage discontinued, Act of February 12, 1873.

Minor Coins.

FIVE-CENT, (*nickel*).—Authorized to be coined, Act of May 16, 1866. Weight, 77.16 grains, composed of 75 per cent. copper and 25 per cent. nickel.

THREE-CENT, (*nickel*).—Authorized to be coined, Act of March 3, 1865. Weight, 30 grains, composed of 75 per cent. copper and 25 per cent. nickel.

TWO-CENT, (*bronze*).—Authorized to be coined, Act of April 22, 1864. Weight, 96 grains, composed of 95 per cent. copper and 5 per cent. tin and zinc. Coinage discontinued, Act of February 12, 1873.

CENT, (*copper*).—Authorized to be coined, Act of April 2, 1792. Weight, 264 grains. Weight changed, Act of January 14, 1793, to 208 grains. Weight changed by proclamation of the President, January 26, 1796, in conformity with Act of March 3, 1795, to 168 grains. Coinage discontinued, Act of February 21, 1857.

CENT, (*nickel*).—Authorized to be coined, Act of February 21, 1857. Weight, 72 grains, composed of 88 per cent. copper and 12 per cent. nickel. Coinage discontinued, Act of April 22, 1864.

CENT, (*bronze*).—Coinage authorized, Act of April

22, 1864. Weight, 48 grains, composed of 95 per cent. copper and 5 per cent. tin and zinc.

HALF-CENT, (*copper*).—Authorized to be coined, Act of April 2, 1792. Weight, 132 grains. Weight changed, Act of January 14, 1793, to 104 grains. Weight changed by proclamation of the President, January 26, 1796, in conformity with Act of March 3, 1795, to 84 grains. Coinage discontinued, Act of February 21, 1857.

(G).—The Ratios of Gold to Silver from 1760 to 1833.

Years.	Pure gold to pure silver.	Years.	Pure gold to pure silver.	Years.	Pure gold to pure silver.
1760	1 to 14.29	1785	1 to 15.21	1810	1 to 16.15
1761	1 to 13.94	1786	1 to 14.89	1811	1 to 15.72
1762	1 to 14.63	1787	1 to 14.83	1812	1 to 15.04
1763	1 to 14.71	1788	1 to 14.71	1813	1 to 14.53
1764	1 to 14.91	1789	1 to 14.89	1814	1 to 15.85
1765	1 to 14.69	1790	1 to 15.01	1815	1 to 16.30
1766	1 to 14.41	1791	1 to 14.95	1816	1 to 13.64
1767	1 to 14.45	1792	1 to 14.43	1817	1 to 15.58
1768	1 to 14.58	1793	1 to 15.01	1818	1 to 15.42
1769	1 to 14.45	1794	1 to 15.32	1819	1 to 15.82
1770	1 to 14.35	1795	1 to 14.77	1820	1 to 15.71
1771	1 to 14.36	1796	1 to 14.77	1821	1 to 15.98
1772	1 to 14.19	1797	1 to 15.45	1822	1 to 15.91
1773	1 to 14.73	1798	1 to 15.45	1823	1 to 15.91
1774	1 to 15.05	1799	1 to 14.29	1824	1 to 15.64
1775	1 to 14.62	1800	1 to 14.81	1825	1 to 15.69
1776	1 to 14.34	1801	1 to 14.47	1826	1 to 15.69
1777	1 to 14.04	1802	1 to 15.23	1827	1 to 15.77
1778	1 to 14.34	1803	1 to 14.47	1828	1 to 15.77
1779	1 to 14.89	1804	1 to 14.67	1829	1 to 15.95
1780	1 to 14.43	1805	1 to 15.14	1830	1 to 15.73
1781	1 to 13.33	1806	1 to 14.25	1831	1 to 15.73
1782	1 to 13.54	1807	1 to 14.46	1832	1 to 15.73
1783	1 to 13.78	1808	1 to 14.79	1833	1 to 15.93
1784	1 to 14.90	1809	1 to 16.25		

NOTE.—The highest value of silver compared with gold, from 1760 to 1833, was in 1781, when 13.33 ounces of the former were equal to one of the latter. In 1809 it required 16¼ ounces of silver to purchase an ounce of gold; the difference represents a change of 14½ per cent. Taking 1781 as the year of the highest relative valuation of silver and the average of the first seven months of 1876 as the lowest, shows a change within a period of 95 years of 34 per cent.

(H).—Table showing the yearly averages of the price of silver from 1834 to 1876, and the corresponding relative values of gold to silver, (prepared from quotations furnished by Pixley and Abell, London.)

Year.	Price per ounce British standard.	Price per ounce, United States standard, in United States gold coin.	Value of a silver dollar of 412½ grains.	Relative value of gold to silver.
	Pence.	*Cents.*	*Cents.*	
1834	59 5/16	118.25	101.62	1 to 15.73
1835	59 1/16	117.76	101.20	1 to 15.79
1836	60	118.37	101.72	1 to 15.71
1837	59 9/16	117.51	100.98	1 to 15.83
1838	59 1/2	117.39	100.88	1 to 15.85
1839	60 3/8	119.11	102.36	1 to 15.61
1840	60 3/8	119.11	102.36	1 to 15.61
1841	60 1/16	118.50	101.83	1 to 15.70
1842	59 7/16	117.26	100.77	1 to 15.86
1843	59 3/16	116.77	100.34	1 to 15.93
1844	59 1/2	117.39	100.88	1 to 15.85
1845	59 1/4	116.90	100.46	1 to 15.91
1846	59 5/16	117.02	100.56	1 to 15.89
1847	59 11/16	117.76	101.20	1 to 15.79
1848	59 1/2	117.39	100.88	1 to 15.85
1849	59 3/4	117.88	101.30	1 to 15.78
1850	60 1/16	118.50	101.83	1 to 15.70
1851	61	120.35	103.42	1 to 15.46
1852	60 1/2	119.36	102.57	1 to 15.58
1853	61 1/2	121.33	104.26	1 to 15.33
1854	61 1/2	121.33	104.26	1 to 15.33
1855	61 5/16	120.96	103.95	1 to 15.38
1856	61 5/16	120.96	103.95	1 to 15.38
1857	61 3/4	121.83	104.69	1 to 15.27
1858	61 5/16	120.96	103.95	1 to 15.38
1859	62 1/16	122.44	105.22	1 to 15.19
1860	61 11/16	121.70	104.58	1 to 15.28
1861	60 13/16	119.98	103.10	1 to 15.50
1862	61 7/16	121.21	104.16	1 to 15.35

(H).—*Continued.*

Year.	Price per ounce British standard.	Price per ounce, United States standard, in United States gold coin.	Value of a silver dollar of 412½ grains.	Relative value of gold to silver.
	Pence.	*Cents.*	*Cents.*	
1863	61 3/8	121.09	104.06	1 to 15.36
1864	61 3/8	121.09	104.06	1 to 15.36
1865	61 1/16	120.47	103.52	1 to 15.44
1866	61 1/8	120.59	103.63	1 to 15.42
1867	60 9/16	119.48	102.67	1 to 15.57
1868	60 1/2	119.36	102.57	1 to 15.58
1869	60 7/16	119.24	102.47	1 to 15.60
1870	60 9/16	119.48	102.67	1 to 15.57
1871	60 1/2	119.36	102.57	1 to 15.58
1872	60 5/16	118.99	102.25	1 to 15.63
1873	59 1/4	116.90	100.46	1 to 15.91
1874	58 5/16	115.04	98.86	1 to 16.17
1875	56 7/8	112.21	96.43	1 to 16.58
1876	52 3/4	104.07	89.22	1 to 17.87

APPENDIX. 163

(I).—STATEMENT OF COINAGE FROM THE ORGANIZATION OF THE MINT TO THE CLOSE OF THE FISCAL YEAR ENDED JUNE 30, 1877.

Gold Coinage.

Period.	Double-eagles.	Eagles.	Half-eagles.	Quarter-eagles.	Three dollars.	Dollars.
1793 to 1795		$27,950	$43,535			
1796		69,340	30,980	$2,407.50		
1797		83,230	18,045	2,147.50		
1798		79,740	124,335	1,535.00		
1799		174,830	37,255	1,200.00		
1800		259,650	58,110			
1801		292,540	130,030			
1802		150,900	265,880	6,530.00		
1803		89,790	167,530	1,057.50		
1804		97,950	152,375	8,317.50		
1805			165,915	4,452.50		
1806			320,465	4,040.00		
1807			420,465	17,030.00		
1808			277,890	6,775.00		
1809			169,375			
1810			501,435			
1811			497,905			
1812			290,435			
1813			477,140			
1814			77,270			
1815			3,175			

(I).—Gold Coinage—Continued.

Period.	Double-eagles.	Eagles.	Half-eagles.	Quarter-eagles.	Three dollars.	Dollars.
1816						
1817						
1818			$242,940			
1819			258,615			
1820			1,319,030			
1821			173,205	$16,120.00		
1822			88,980			
1823			72,425			
1824			86,700	6,500.00		
1825			145,300	11,085.00		
1826			90,345	1,900.00		
1827			124,565	7,000.00		
1828			140,145			
1829			287,210	8,507.50		
1830			631,755	11,350.00		
1831			702,970	11,300.00		
1832			787,435	11,000.00		
1833			968,150	10,400.00		
1834			3,660,845	293,425.00		
1835			1,857,670	328,505.00		
1836			2,765,735	1,369,965.00		
1837		$72,000	1,035,605	112,700.00		
1838		382,480	1,600,285	137,310.00		
1839		473,380	802,745	170,660.00		
1840			1,048,360	153,562.50		

APPENDIX.

Year					
1841		656,310	54,562.50		
1842		1,089,070	89,770.00		
1843		2,506,240	1,327,132.50		
1844		1,250,610	89,345.00		
1845		736,530	276,277.50		
1846		1,018,750	279,272.50		
1847		14,337,640	482,060.00		
1848		1,813,340	98,612.50		
1849		6,775,180	111,147.50		$936,789
1850	$26,225,220	3,489,510	895,547.50		511,301
1851	48,043,100	4,393,280	3,867,337.50		3,658,820
1852	44,860,520	2,811,060	3,283,827.50		2,201,145
1853	26,646,520	2,522,530	3,519,615.00		4,384,149
1854	18,052,340	2,305,760	1,896,397.50	$491,214	1,657,012
1855	24,636,820	1,487,010	600,700.00	171,465	824,883
1856	30,277,560	1,484,900	1,213,117.50	181,530	1,788,996
1857	14,056,300	129,160	320,465.00	38,496	593,532
1858	28,038,880	629,900	515,632.50	66,177	230,361
1859	16,236,720	146,000	213,010.00	34,572	259,065
1860	15,458,800	342,130	128,980.00	61,206	93,215
1861	59,316,420	552,050	338,440.00	18,216	15,521
1862	36,247,500	972,990	3,208,122.50	17,355	1,799,259
1863	20,387,720	126,580	62,475.00	117	1,950
1864	21,465,640	85,800	23,185.00	16,470	6,750
1865	24,879,600	93,750	30,502.50	10,065	7,225
1866	27,494,900	376,100	122,975.00	12,090	7,130
1867	27,925,400	51,150	73,062.50	7,875	5,225
1868	17,705,800	155,500	74,125.00	14,700	10,550
1869	21,270,500	209,850	105,862.50	7,575	5,925
1870	22,018,480	89,130	35,137.50	10,605	9,335

(I).—Gold Coinage—Continued.

Period.	Double-eagles.	Eagles.	Half-eagles.	Quarter-eagles.	Three dollars.	Dollars.
1871	$20,919,240	$163,250	$158,625	$53,400.00	$4,020	$3,940
1872	19,798,500	254,600	243,700	72,575.00	6,090	1,030
1873	34,765,500	204,650	237,525	39,062.50	75	2,525
1874	48,283,900	383,480	809,780	516,150.00	125,460	323,920
1875	32,748,140	599,840	203,655	2,250.00	60	20
1876	37,896,720	153,610	71,800	53,052.50	135	3,645
1877	43,941,700	56,200	67,835	5,780.00	4,464	2,220
Total.	809,598,440	56,707,220	69,412,815	26,795,750.00	1,300,032	19,345,438

Silver Coinage.

Period.	Trade dollars	Dollars.	Half Dollars.	Quarter-dollars.	Twenty-c'ts.	Dimes.	Half-dimes.	Three-cents.
1793 to 1795		$204,791	$161,572.00	$1,473.50		$2,213.50	$4,320.80	
1796		72,920	1,959.00	63.00		2,526.10	511.50	
1797		7,776				2,755.00	2,226.35	
1798		327,536						
1799		423,515						
1800		220,920				2,176.00	1,200.00	
1801		54,454	15,144.50			3,464.00	1,695.50	

APPENDIX.

Year				
1802	41,650	14,945.00		
1803	66,064	15,857.50		
1804	19,570	78,259.50	1,684.50	
1805	321	105,861.00	30,348.50	
1806		419,788.00	51,531.00	
1807		525,788.00	55,160.75	1,097.50
1808		684,300.00		3,304.00
1809		702,905.00		826.50
1810		638,138.00		12,078.00
1811		601,822.00		
1812		814,029.50		16,500.00
1813		620,951.50		4,471.00
1814		519,537.50		635.50
1815				6,518.00
1816		23,575.00	17,308.00	
1817		607,783.50	5,000.75	42,150.00
1818		980,161.00		
1819		1,104,000.00	90,293.50	
1820		375,561.00	36,000.00	94,258.70
1821		652,898.50	31,861.00	118,651.20
1822		779,786.50	54,212.75	10,000.00
1823		847,100.00	16,020.00	44,000.00
1824		1,752,477.00	4,450.00	
1825		1,471,583.00		51,000.00
1826		2,002,090.00	42,000.00	
1827		2,746,700.00		121,500.00
1828		1,537,600.00	1,000.00	12,500.00
1829		1,856,078.00	25,500.00	77,000.00	61,500.00
1830		2,382,400.00		51,000.00	62,000.00
1831		2,936,830.00	99,500.00	77,135.00	62,135.00

(I).—Silver Coinage—Continued.

Period	Trade dollars	Dollars	Half Dollars	Quarter-dollars	Twenty-c'ts	Dimes	Half-dimes	Three-cents
1832			$2,398,500.00	$80,000.00		$52,250.00	$48,250.00	
1833			2,603,000.00	39,000.00		48,500.00	68,500.00	
1834			3,206,002.00	71,500.00		63,500.00	74,000.00	
1835			2,676,003.00	488,000.00		141,000.00	138,000.00	
1836		$1,000	3,273,100.00	118,000.00		119,000.00	95,000.00	
1837			1,814,910.00	63,100.00		104,200.00	113,800.00	
1838			1,773,000.00	208,000.00		239,493.00	112,750.00	
1839		300	1,717,280.50	122,786.50		229,471.50	106,457.50	
1840		61,005	1,145,054.00	153,331.75		253,358.00	113,954.25	
1841		173,000	355,500.00	143,000.00		363,000.00	98,250.00	
1842		184,618	1,484,882.00	214,250.00		390,750.00	58,250.00	
1843		165,100	3,056,000.00	403,400.00		152,000.00	58,250.00	
1844		20,000	1,885,500.00	290,300.00		7,250.00	32,500.00	
1845		24,500	1,341,500.00	230,500.00		198,500.00	78,200.00	
1846		169,600	2,257,000.00	127,500.00		3,130.00	1,350.00	
1847		140,750	1,870,000.00	280,500.00		24,500.00	63,700.00	
1848		15,000	1,880,000.00	36,500.00		45,150.00	63,400.00	
1849		62,600	1,781,000.00	85,000.00		113,900.00	72,450.00	
1850		47,500	1,341,500.00	150,700.00		244,150.00	82,250.00	
1851		1,300	301,375.00	62,000.00		142,650.00	82,050.00	$185,022.00
1852		1,100	110,565.00	68,265.00		196,550.00	63,625.00	559,905.00
1853		46,110	2,430,354.00	4,146,555.00		1,327,301.00	785,251.00	342,000.00
1854		33,140	4,111,000.00	3,466,000.00		624,000.00	365,000.00	20,130.00
1855		26,000	2,284,725.00	861,350.00		207,500.00	117,500.00	4,170.00
1856		63,500	1,903,500.00	2,129,500.00		696,000.00	299,000.00	43,740.00

APPENDIX.

Year								
1857		94,000	114,000.00	583,000.00		489,000.00	197,000.00	37,980.00
1858			4,430,000.00	3,019,750.00		226,000.00	327,000.00	41,400.00
1859		288,500	4,005,500.00	1,428,000.00		229,000.00	195,000.00	16,440.00
1860		600,530	1,627,400.00	339,450.00		98,600.00	96,500.00	7,950.00
1861		559,900	959,650.00	771,550.00		167,300.00	139,350.00	18,256.50
1862		1,750	1,785,425.00	730,937.50		158,405.00	117,627.50	2,803.80
1863		31,400	983,630.00	113,965.00		34,071.00	8,223.00	11.10
1864		23,170	483,985.00	22,492.50		14,037.00	4,518.50	618.00
1865		32,900	553,100.00	27,650.00		17,160.00	4,880.00	679.50
1866		58,550	579,525.00	9,712.50		21,065.00	10,732.50	141.00
1867		57,900	897,450.00	18,175.00		13,670.00	435.00	120.00
1868		54,800	946,750.00	37,475.00		73,315.00	24,290.00	151.50
1869		231,350	561,675.00	23,137.50		23,905.00	527.50	115.50
1870		588,308	1,009,375.00	23,047.50		98,185.00	48,222.50	129.75
1871		657,929	1,242,771.00	29,971.75		10,707.50	14,396.25	61.05
1872		1,112,961	1,486,492.50	55,096.25		222,471.50	152,751.75	25.50
1873		977,150	1,199,775.00	174,362.50		419,040.00	175,442.50	
1874	$3,588,900		1,438,930.00	458,515.50		497,255.80		
1875	5,697,500		2,853,500.00	623,950.00	$5,858.00	889,560.00		
1876	6,132,050		4,985,525.00	4,106,262.50	263,560.00	3,639,105.00		
1877	9,162,900		9,746,350.00	7,584,175.00	1,440.00	2,055,070.00		
Total,	24,581,350	8,045,838	118,869,540.50	34,774,121.50	270,858.00	16,141,786.30	4,906,946.90	1,281,850.20

170

Period	MINOR COINAGE					TOTAL COINAGE		
	Five-cents.	Three-cts.	Two-cts.	Cents.	Half-cts.	Gold.	Silver.	Minor.	Total.
1793 to 1795				$10,660.33	$712.67	$71,485.00	$370,683.80	$11,373.00	$453,541.80
1796				9,747.00	577.40	102,727.50	79,077.50	10,324.40	192,129.40
1797				8,975.10	535.24	103,422.50	12,591.45	9,510.34	125,524.29
1798				9,797.00		205,610.00	330,291.00	9,797.00	545,698.00
1799				9,045.85	60.83	213,285.00	423,515.00	9,106.68	645,906.68
1800				28,221.75	1,057.65	317,760.00	224,296.00	29,279.40	571,335.40
1801				13,628.37		422,570.00	74,758.00	13,628.37	510,956.37
1802				34,351.00	71.83	423,310.00	58,343.00	34,422.83	516,075.83
1803				24,713.53	489.50	258,377.50	87,118.00	25,203.03	370,698.53
1804				7,568.38	5,276.56	258,642.50	100,340.50	12,844.94	371,827.94
1805				9,411.16	4,072.32	170,367.50	149,388.50	13,483.48	333,239.48
1806				3,480.00	1,780.00	324,505.00	471,319.00	5,260.00	801,084.00
1807				7,272.21	2,380.00	437,495.00	597,448.75	9,652.21	1,044,595.96
1808				11,090.00	2,000.00	284,665.00	684,300.00	13,090.00	982,055.00
1809				2,228.67	5,772.86	169,375.00	707,376.00	8,001.53	884,752.53
1810				14,585.00	1,075.00	501,435.00	638,773.50	15,660.00	1,155,868.50
1811				2,180.25	315.70	497,905.00	608,340.00	2,495.95	1,108,740.95
1812				10,755.00		290,435.00	814,029.50	10,755.00	1,115,219.50
1813				4,180.00		477,140.00	620,951.50	4,180.00	1,102,271.50
1814				3,578.30		77,270.00	561,687.50	3,578.30	642,535.80
1815						3,175.00	17,308.00		20,483.00
1816				28,209.82			28,575.75	28,209.82	56,785.57
1817				39,484.00			607,783.50	39,484.00	647,267.50
1818				31,670.00		242,940.00	1,070,454.50	31,670.00	1,345,064.50
1819				26,710.00		258,615.00	1,140,000.00	26,710.00	1,425,325.00
1820				44,075.50		1,319,030.00	501,680.70	44,075.50	1,864,786.20
1821				3,890.00		189,325.00	825,762.45	3,890.00	1,018,977.45
1822				20,723.39		88,080.00	805,806.50	20,723.39	915,509.89
1823						72,425.00	895,550.00		967,975.00
1824				12,620.00		93,200.00	1,752,477.00	12,620.00	1,858,297.00
1825				14,611.00	315.00	156,385.00	1,564,583.00	14,926.00	1,735,894.00
1826				15,174.25	1,170.00	92,245.00	2,002,090.00	16,344.25	2,110,679.25
1827				23,577.32		131,565.00	2,869,200.00	23,577.32	3,024,342.32

APPENDIX.

Year							
1828	22,606.24	3,030.00		140,145.00	1,575,600.00	25,636.24	1,741,381.24
1829	14,145.00	2,435.00		295,717.50	1,994,578.00	16,580.00	2,306,875.50
1830	17,115.00		11.00	643,105.00	2,495,400.00	17,115.00	3,155,620.00
1831	33,592.60			714,270.00	3,175,600.00	33,603.60	3,923,473.60
1832	23,620.00			798,435.00	2,579,000.00	23,620.00	3,401,055.00
1833	27,390.00	770.00		978,550.00	2,759,000.00	28,160.00	3,765,710.00
1834	18,551.00	600.00		3,954,270.00	3,415,002.00	19,151.00	7,388,423.00
1835	38,784.00	705.00		2,186,175.00	3,443,003.00	39,489.00	5,668,667.00
1836	21,110.00	1,990.00		4,135,700.00	3,666,100.00	23,100.00	7,764,900.00
1837	55,583.00			1,148,305.00	2,096,010.00	55,583.00	3,299,898.00
1838	63,702.00			1,809,595.00	2,333,243.00	63,702.00	4,206,540.00
1839	31,286.61			1,355,885.00	2,176,296.00	31,286.61	3,563,467.61
1840	24,627.00			1,675,302.50	1,726,703.00	24,627.00	3,426,632.50
1841	15,973.67			1,091,597.50	1,132,750.00	15,973.67	2,240,321.17
1842	23,833.90			1,834,170.00	2,332,750.00	23,833.90	4,190,753.90
1843	24,283.20			8,108,797.50	3,834,750.00	24,283.20	11,967,830.70
1844	23,987.52			5,428,230.00	2,235,550.00	23,987.52	7,687,767.52
1845	38,948.04			3,756,447.50	1,873,200.00	38,948.04	5,668,595.54
1846	41,208.00			4,034,177.50	2,558,580.00	41,208.00	6,633,965.50
1847	61,836.69			20,221,385.00	2,379,450.00	61,836.69	22,662,671.69
1848	64,157.99			3,775,512.50	2,040,050.00	64,157.99	5,879,720.49
1849	41,785.00		199.32	9,007,761.50	2,114,950.00	41,984.32	11,164,695.82
1850	44,268.44		199.06	31,981,738.50	1,866,100.00	44,467.50	33,892,306.00
1851	98,897.07		738.36	62,614,492.50	774,397.00	99,635.43	63,488,524.93
1852	50,630.94			56,846,187.50	999,410.00	50,630.94	57,896,228.44
1853	66,411.31	648.47		39,377,909.00	9,077,571.00	67,059.78	48,522,539.78
1854	42,361.56	276.79		25,915,918.50	8,619,270.00	42,638.35	34,577,826.85
1855	15,748.29	282.50		28,977,968.00	3,501,245.00	16,030.79	32,495,243.79
1856	26,904.63	202.15		36,697,768.50	5,135,240.00	27,106.78	41,860,115.28
1857	63,334.56	175.90		15,811,563.00	1,477,000.00	63,510.46	17,352,073.46
1858	234,000.00			30,253,725.50	8,040,730.00	234,000.00	38,528,455.50
1859	307,000.00			17,296,077.00	6,187,400.00	307,000.00	23,790,477.00
1860	342,000.00			16,445,476.00	2,769,920.00	342,000.00	19,557,396.00
1861	101,660.00			60,693,237.00	2,605,700.00	101,660.00	63,400,597.00
1862	116,000.00			45,532,386.50	2,812,401.50	116,000.00	48,460,788.00
1863	478,450.00			20,695,852.00	1,174,092.80	478,450.00	22,348,394.80
1864	427,350.00			21,649,345.00	548,214.10	463,800.00	22,661,359.10
1865	541,800.00			25,107,217.50	636,308.00	1,183,330.00	26,926,855.50
	$05,930.00	$36,450.00	535,600.00				

(I.)—Continued.

Period	MINOR COINAGE.					TOTAL COINAGE.			
	Five-cents.	Three-cts.	Two-cts.	Cents.	Half-cts.	Gold.	Silver.	Minor.	Total.
1866	$66,240.00	$270,270.00	122,980.00	$187,680.00		$28,313,945.00	$680,264.50	$646,570.00	$29,640,779.50
1867	1,562,500.00	133,410.00	69,880.00	113,750.00		28,217,187.50	986,871.00	1,879,540.00	31,083,598.50
1868	1,445,100.00	108,390.00	61,330.00	98,565.00		18,114,425.00	1,136,750.00	1,713,385.00	20,964,560.00
1869	1,101,250.00	64,380.00	34,615.00	78,810.00		21,828,637.50	840,746.50	1,279,055.00	23,948,439.00
1870	487,500.00	42,690.00	22,890.00	58,365.00		22,257,312.50	1,707,253.50	611,445.00	24,636,011.00
1871	171,950.00	27,630.00	22,105.00	62,075.00		21,302,475.00	1,955,905.25	283,760.00	23,542,140.25
1872	89,200.00	18,330.00	6,170.00	9,320.00		20,376,495.00	3,029,834.05	123,020.00	23,529,349.05
1873	352,400.00	34,320.00		107,330.00		35,249,337.50	2,945,795.50	494,050.00	38,689,183.00
1874	244,350.00	29,640.00		137,935.00		50,442,690.00	5,983,661.30	411,925.00	56,838,216.30
1875	94,650.00	12,540.00		123,185.00		33,553,965.00	10,070,368.00	230,375.00	43,854,708.00
1876	132,700.00	7,560.00		120,090.00		38,178,962.50	19,126,592.50	260,350.00	57,565,815.00
1877	25,250.00			36,915.00		44,078,199.00	28,549,935.00	62,165.00	72,690,299.00
Total.	5,773,090.00	855,090.00	912,020.00	5,304,577.44	39,926.11	983,159,695.00	208,872,291.40	12,884,703.55	1,204,916,689.95

APPENDIX.

RECAPITULATION BY PERIODS OF CHANGES IN STANDARD.

Period.	Standard.	Gold.	Silver (full legal tender).	Silver (over-valued and limited legal tender).	Minor Coinage.
1792 to 1834	Gold and silver at relative valuation of 1 to 15,	$11,825,890.00	$36,275,077.90		$658,591.58
1834 to 1853	Gold and silver at relative valuation of 1 to 15.98+,	224,965,730.00	42,938,294.00		787,885.81
1853 to 1873	Gold and silver at 1 to 15.98+, silver represented by the dollar,	544,864,921.00	5,538,948.00 Trade dollars* (no legal tender).	$57,443,769.20	9,979,361.16
1873 to 1877	Gold standard, silver subsidiary,	201,503,154.00	24,581,350.00	42,094,852.30	1,458,865.00

* Trade dollars were legal tenders to the amount of five dollars until July 22, 1876.

www.ingramcontent.com/pod-product-compliance
Lightning Source LLC
Chambersburg PA
CBHW020250170426
43202CB00008B/299